Archaeology and Forestry in Ireland

Gina Johnson

An Chomhairle Oidhreachta   The Heritage Council

First published in 1998 by
The Heritage Council,
Kilkenny,
Ireland

ISBN 1393-0808
The Heritage Council of Ireland Series
ISBN 1 901137 02 3

Production and layout by Gina Johnson

Edited by Charles Mount

Cover Design by B. Magee Design

Typeset and printed in Ireland by Cahill Printers Ltd.

Price: £7.00

Contents

T

Contents

List of Figures

Abbreviations Used in Text

AGS	Afforestation Grant Scheme
ALS	Afforestable Land Survey
CADW	Welsh Historic Monuments
CAP	Common Agricultural Policy
COFORD	The Council for Forest Research and Development
D/AFF	Department of Agriculture, Food and Forestry
D/AHGI	Department of Arts, Heritage, the Gaeltacht and the Islands
D/ANI	Department of Agriculture for Northern Ireland
D/MNR	Department of the Marine and Natural Resources
D/OE	Department of the Environment
D/OENI	Department of the Environment for Northern Ireland
EIA	Environmental Impact Assessment
ESRI	Economic and Social Research Institute
FAO	Food and Agriculture Organisation
FÁS	Foras Áiseanna Saothair
FIRST	Forest Institute of Remote Sensing Technology
FPS	Forest Premium Scheme
GIS	Geographical Information System
GSI	Geological Survey of Ireland
GTO	Grants to Owners
HEM	Historic Environment Manager
IAPA	Irish Association of Professional Archaeologists
ICMSA	Irish Creamery Milk Suppliers Association
IFA	Irish Farmers Association
IFIC	Irish Forest Industry Chain
IFS	Indicative Forest Strategy
IPCC	Irish Peatland Conservancy Council
ITGA	Irish Timber Growers Association
NHA	Natural Heritage Area
NMA	National Monuments Act/s
NMHPS	National Monuments and Historic Properties Service
OP	Operational Programme (for Agriculture, Rural Development and Forestry)
OPW	Office of Public Works
OS	Ordnance Survey
RCAHMS	Royal Commission of the Archaeological and Historic Monuments of Scotland
REPS	Rural Environmental Protection Scheme
SAC	Special Areas for Conservation
SIC	Society of Irish Foresters
SMR	Sites and Monuments Record
SPAs	Special Protection Areas
UCC	University College Cork
UCD	University College Dublin
UFA	United Farmers Association
UK	United Kingdom
WGS	Woodland Grant Scheme

Acknowledgements

The generous assistance, information and advice received from the following is gratefully acknowledged:

Michael Bulfin, *Teagasc*
Emmet Byrnes, *Department of Archaeology, UCD*
Rose Cleary, *Department of Archaeology, UCC*
Tom Condit, *National Monuments and Historic Properties Service*
Gabriel Cooney, *Department of Archaeology, UCD*
John Cronin, *Cork Archaeological Survey, UCC*
Brian Duffy, *National Monuments and Historic Properties Service*
Claire Foley, *Department of the Environment, Northern Ireland*
Glenasack Forestry Ltd, Co. Cork
Michael Gibbons
Matthew Kelleher
Seán Kirwan, *Department of Arts, Heritage, the Gaeltacht and the Islands*
Lesley Macinnes, *Historic Scotland*
Tim McCarthy, *Foraiste don bPobail*
John McLoughlin, *Coillte Teoranta*
Seán Murphy, Derreenaling, Co. Cork
Tom O'Byrne, *Irish Wildlife Federation*
Ray Ó Coinneadagh
Pat O'Connell, *Forest Service, Cork*
Terry O'Regan, *Landscape Alliance Ireland*
Denis Power, *Limerick Archaeological Survey*
Andre Q. Berry, *Clwyd Archaeological Services, Wales*
Rachael Uí Riorda, *Údarás na Gaeltachta, Ballyvourney*
Lee Snodgrass
Caroline Wickham-Jones
Peter Woodman, *Department of Archaeology, UCC*
Timothy Yarnell, *The Forestry Commission, Edinburgh*
The staff of the Cork Archaeological Survey, UCC
The staff of the Department of Archaeology, UCC

Thanks are due, in particular, to Gabriel Cooney, John Cronin and Seán Kirwan for advice and discussion, to Denis Power for assistance throughout the course of the project, and to the Cork Archaeological Survey, UCC, for facilitating research and compilation of the project.

Foreword

The former National Heritage Council, under the chairmanship of Lord Killanin, commissioned Gina Johnson to prepare a report on Archaeology and Forestry in Ireland. On receipt of the final report from Ms. Johnson by the Heritage Council (established on a statutory basis by Minister Michael D. Higgins, TD., in July 1995), the Council decided that it should be published to make the valuable information and recommendations contained in the report available to the many agencies and individuals with an interest in the impact of forestry on archaeology.

Ireland has the most ambitious forestry programme in Europe, and in the State Strategy on Forestry it is proposed to increase planting by 25,000 ha per annum to the year 2000, and by 20,000 ha per annum to the year 2030. The Heritage Council recognises the need for policies in regard to the beneficial development of forestry in relation to the environmental and manmade heritage. This publication is intended as a review of the existing structures with the author's recommendations to aid in the development of future policy.

With the increased interest and awareness of environmental and heritage issues, it is hoped that this report will make a positive contribution to the continuing development of sustainable development strategies at all levels in Ireland.

Freda Rountree
Chairperson, March 1998

Réamhrá

Rinne an IarChomhairle Oidhreachta Náisiúnta a raibh Tiarna Killanin mar chathaoirleach uirthi Gina Johnson a chomisiún chun tuairisc a ráiteach ar Sheandalaíocht agus ar Fhoraoiseacht in Éirinn. Fuar An Chomhairle Oidhreachta (a bunaíodh ar bhun reachtúil i 1995) an tuairisc seo agus tugadh cothram le data í ina dhiaidh sin lena foilsiú sa chaoi go mbeadh an t-eolas agus na moltaí luachmhara atá sa tuairisc le fáil ag go leor gníomhaireachtaí agus ag daoine aonair a bhfuil suim acu in éifeacht na foraoiseachta ar an tseandalaíocht.

Is ag Éirinn atá an clár foraoiseachta is uaillmhianaí san Eoraip agus molann an chaipéis faoi straitéis foraoise náisiúnta "Growing for the Future" (Seirbhís Foraoise, 1996) go ndéanfaí méadú de 25,000 ha sa bhliain ar an méid crann a chuirfí go dtí an bhliain 2000 agus de 20,000 ha sa bhliain go dtí an bhliain 2030. Tuigeann an Chomhairle Oidhreachta go dteastaíonn polasaithe maidir le forbairt a rachaidh chun tairbhe den fhoraoiseacht ó thaobh na timpeallachta agus na hoidhreachta saorga de. Tá sí mar aidhm ag an bhfoilseachán seo athbhreithniú a dhéanamh ar struchtúir atá ann cheana féin le moltaí an údair mar chúnamh san athbhreithniú foirmealta a bheidh ann tar éis dóibh a bheith curtha i bhfeidhm ar feadh cúig bliana.

Mar go bhfuil níos mó suime ag daoine i nithe a bhaineann leis an timpeallacht agus leis an oidhreacht agus go bhfuil níos mó eolas acu orthu, táthar ag súil go gcuirfidh an tuairisc seo go dearfach le straitéisí forbartha leanúnacha ag gach leibhéal in Éirinn.

Freda Rountree
Cathaoirleach, Márta 1998

Preface

Archaeology is an essential element of Irish culture and must be protected and managed for future generations. Afforestation poses a greater threat to archaeology than any other rural land-use. Planting trends have changed considerably in the past five years and forestry is now distributed on a wide variety of soil-types in a wide range of landscapes. The onus is on the archaeological and forestry authorities to ensure identification and protection of sites threatened by afforestation.

The original intention of this research was to explore the impact of afforestation on archaeology in the marginal zones of Ireland where planting had been concentrated. Evidence, from Ireland and elsewhere, suggested that forestry was damaging and destroying archaeological sites at an unprecedented rate. Archaeology in marginal upland areas and previously undeveloped land appeared to be most at risk with large sections of prominent mountain ranges and valuable boglands already planted.

Planting patterns and farming practices have changed in recent years, however, and the threat to archaeology has become even more widespread and more complex. Afforestation now poses a greater threat to archaeology than most other rural land-uses. The systems and processes involved in the administration of archaeology and forestry are continuously developing and changing and are constantly forcing new issues to be considered. As such, it was felt that a broad-based, comprehensive investigation of the industry and its relationship with archaeology was warranted to allow for an overall assessment of the situation.

Objections to large-scale afforestation of the countryside have been voiced by rural community action groups, farmers, environmental groups and more recently by archaeologists. While some sectors have successfully organised their protests, utilising media exposure and political pressure to express their concerns, the case for archaeology is as yet fragmentary. The primary role of this research, therefore, was to update the situation *vis-à-vis* archaeology and forestry and to draw together some of the available evidence.

Two central assumptions are maintained throughout the report: 1) that archaeology is a valuable and irreplaceable resource, and 2) that forestry, provided it is planned as part of an inclusive management scheme, can be a positive aspect of the countryside. While archaeology and forestry may sometimes appear to be vying with each other for superior status, there are mutual benefits to be gained from a co-operative approach to their promotion and management. The two subjects are explored here in the broader context in which they exist, that is, their relationships with rural communities, the environment and natural habitats, the landscape and the Irish economy.

There are practical difficulties involved in responding to any rural development which has the potential to impact on archaeology. Comprehensive legal protection of archaeological sites and monuments is now in place but there is a fundamental problem with implementing this protection — there is no policy or system in place for the management of archaeological sites and monuments at a local or regional level. Therefore, the impact of any new land-use has to be addressed from a variety of aspects starting with what is regarded as 'archaeology', how to identify it, and how to protect and manage it. Communication between archaeology and other sectors involved with land and land-use issues must also be improved considerably. The centralised system in place for dealing with archaeological matters, however, cannot always provide a practical response to rural developments, in this case, forestry.

Executive Summary

Ireland is particularly rich in archaeological sites and monuments which form a central component of Irish Heritage. These sites, however, can be affected at any stage in the forest cycle; planting preparation, forest establishment, maturity, and harvesting, all pose dangers to sites within the plantation. The distribution of afforestation in Ireland has increased the threat to archaeological sites and monuments, but the extent of the potential impact is not yet known.

- There are three inter-related stages in protecting archaeological sites from afforestation and the activities associated with it: 1) identifying sites and monuments, 2) enforcing their legal protection, and ensuring adherence to the Forest Service guidelines on archaeology and forestry, and 3) planning forestry in such a way that damage to archaeology is minimised and sustaining management plans for the forest environment.

- The extent of the impact of afforestation on archaeological sites is not yet known. Assessment of a sample of archaeological sites known to exist in forestry is required to investigate the extent of the damage to archaeological sites. It would also provide information on which to base management policy and mitigating procedures to reduce the potential impact of afforestation on the archaeological heritage.

- Statutory protection is conferred on archaeological sites that are entered in the Record of Monuments and Places. This lists sites that have previously been identified, but many more remain to be discovered. Over reliance on the Record of Monuments and Places must be avoided and its preliminary status must be emphasised. The lists must be continuously updated and distributed to the Forest Service, the larger forestry companies, and those with control over agricultural/forestry activities in the regions.

- Identifying and protecting unrecorded archaeological sites requires input from professional archaeologists into forestry training and education courses. It also requires a more direct form of contact and consultation between archaeologists and foresters during the planting process.

- The initial risks to archaeological sites could be reduced through consultation with archaeologists and through field-based assessment pre-afforestation. The costs of archaeological assessment must be borne by the developer, but financial assistance from the forestry programme could reasonably be expected for pre-planting inspection of planting proposals.

- To ensure continued protection for archaeological sites in forests, landowners must be actively encouraged to maintain sites free of overgrowth and to ensure protection against accidental damage from machinery, wind-throw, etc. Forest managers should not be financially penalised through the loss of income for protecting archaeological sites. Compensation for such management could be provided by formally including the unplanted 'buffer zone' in the calculation of the forest grant.

- To fully assess the impact of afforestation on archaeological sites, it is necessary to identify those sites that already exist in forestry. An inventory of archaeological sites in existing forestry would allow a more complete assessment of the situation and would facilitate management policies and plans for their future.

- At present, the only form of archaeological survey carried out pre-afforestation is through the Environmental Impact Assessment process. There is some evidence to suggest that the methodologies employed and the standards of practice are not always adequate. Reassessment of the standards of archaeological impact assessment, and the introduction of a code of practice for pre-development surveying are required.

11

- The establishment of an archaeological unit, specifically intended to investigate areas pre-afforestation, would not be capable of responding to current forestry trends. It would, however, be useful for carrying out large-scale pre-afforestation surveys, and for co-ordinating individual assessments of proposed planting areas. In co-operation with the Forest Service, such a unit could be deployed to investigate areas targeted for afforestation by Indicative Forestry Schemes.

- The appointment of regional or local-authority archaeologists would facilitate assessment of planting proposals and site inspections at local level, as well as providing information and advice for local landowners.

- Monitoring of the planting process, by an experienced archaeologist, would provide an opportunity to identify unrecorded sites and allow appropriate action to be taken.

- The National Monuments Acts (1930-1994) provide legal protection for archaeological sites and monuments. The Forest Service guidelines on archaeology and forestry facilitate the implementation of the NMAs. The legislation and guidelines must be enforced in practice, through monitoring and field-based inspection of sites. Regulations regarding archaeology and afforestation need to be introduced to include all planting and not just that which is grant-aided. In order to achieve this, comprehensive ground-level contact between the archaeologists and the forestry sector will have to be formally established.

- Given that Coillte is the largest single landowner in Ireland, the company must be encouraged to employ at least one professional archaeologist to oversee compliance with the Forest Service guidelines, and to assess the condition of sites which already exist within its forestry.

- Querying the presence of archaeological sites in an area to be planted would serve a dual purpose — to identify previously unrecorded sites and to raise awareness of the need to protect archaeological sites from developments such as forestry.

- Management and maintenance of archaeological sites in forestry must be introduced if their long-term survival is to be ensured. Where sites are particularly fragile and/or under threat, specific management procedures must be enforced.

- Unambiguous marking of the protected buffer zone must be introduced and maintained throughout the life cycle of the forest plantation to ensure protection of archaeological sites, particularly during felling operations.

- The landscape context of an archaeological site or group of sites must be considered as part of the normal forest planning.

- A policy of management for archaeological sites in forestry is required to facilitate participation in the development of land-use and landscape policies.

- Archaeology can be considered as an asset within forestry, particularly that which is intended for amenity, recreation and tourism. There must, however, be more active involvement from professional archaeologists to ensure that promotion of sites is carried out in an appropriate manner.

CHAPTER 1

Identifying and Protecting Archaeological Sites

INTRODUCTION
Ireland has an exceptional archaeological heritage which must be protected from all developments including afforestation.

Archaeology is an essential and non-renewable component of Irish culture, heritage and the Irish landscape. Ireland is exceptionally rich in archaeological features with between 150,000 and 200,000 known pre-AD 1700 sites and monuments (Condit 1991, 111). These sites range from substantial monuments (Fig. 1) to fragile traces of human activity (Fig. 2) and settlements (Fig. 3). While the intrinsic value of archaeology is readily accepted, archaeological sites are not always afforded an appropriate status when they come into conflict with other factors. European and Irish legislation, however, now exists to protect archaeology and to promote awareness of the archaeological heritage.

Fig. 1. *The Forrad and Tech Cormaic at Tara, Co. Meath (Discovery Programme).*

Archaeological sites and monuments
Archaeological sites and monuments range from substantial above-ground structures to easily damaged subterranean traces of human activity. While monuments are the most obvious feature of the archaeological heritage, their less visible counterparts generally tend to produce more substantial and informative evidence. In addition, archaeological sites are not necessarily identified or defined by structures. For some periods in prehistory, artefacts are the only remaining indicators of human activity. Archaeological sites

Archaeological sites occur in two general forms: 1) visible structures, such as earthworks, stone monuments, etc. and 2) subterranean features, such as house foundations (Fig. 4), burials and buried earthen or stone features. The distinction is significant because of a tendency for highly visible archaeology to dominate public perception of the subject. While a landowner may be protective of a megalithic structure, for example, he/she may not be aware of the wealth of information lying beneath the soil. 'Low visibility' sites are particularly important since they will normally reveal the more detailed evidence of prehistoric economies, societies, environments and rituals. These sites are usually identified either by chance or by intensive fieldwork programmes designed to search for indicators of their existence. Subterranean features such as pit burials, cist graves, house foundations, or levelled earthworks, cannot be identified easily. A cist grave or a souterrain, for example, might only be discovered when the wheel of a tractor

13

and monuments in Ireland face a relatively new threat in the form of large-scale developments that have the potential to damage or destroy much of the archaeological heritage.

accidentally breaks into the cavity of the structure. Similarly, levelled earthworks or buried earthen or stone features are usually only visible as anomalies in soil colour in ploughed soil or crop growth; these are normally identified through aerial surveying.

Fig. 2. *Hurdle Trackway from Derryoghil, Co. Longford (Barry Raftery).*

For some periods stone, ceramic and metal artefacts are the only surviving indicators of a prehistoric site. There are no known above-ground remains from the Mesolithic period, for example, and therefore all known sites have been discovered either by chance (see, for example, Woodman and O'Brien 1993) or by intensive surveying of buried landscapes (eg. Anderson 1993).

Archaeology also deals with the study of prehistoric animal and plant life and therefore organic remains are essential components of the archaeological record. In addition to evidence for human occupation, settlement and burial, information on past landscapes, climate and environment is only present in buried soils. The microfossil pollen record, which is essential to an understanding of past land-use, landscapes and climate, comes from lake sediments and intact peatbogs; macrofossil plant and animal remains, as well as timber structural remains, can also be preserved in waterlogged soils and bogs.

The two forms of archaeology (visible and buried) will sometimes occur in tandem, with an above-ground structure indicating the presence of subsurface remains. In some cases, house foundations and associated artefacts have been found directly beneath megalithic tombs, for example, Ballyglass, Co. Mayo (Ó Nualláin 1972). Similarly, at Altanagh, Co. Tyrone, four Neolithic pit burials were uncovered during excavation of a megalithic tomb (Williams 1986). While monuments are the most obvious features of the archaeological heritage, the vast bulk of information lies buried in the landscape.

Fig. 3. *Stone enclosures at Carrig Aille, Co. Limerick (Cambridge University Committee for Aerial Photography).*

Fig. 4. *Foundation trench of the Neolithic house at Tankardstown South, Co. Limerick (Margaret Gowen).*

The archaeological record is continuously being added to, through research, archaeological surveys, pre-development assessments and through accidental discovery of artefacts and previously unrecorded sites. Although only a percentage of the archaeological heritage will ever be discovered, the ultimate aim of archaeology is to maximise the information that is available, and to protect and conserve, where possible, the heritage for future generations. In recent years, large-scale developments (for example, road construction, industrial complexes and afforestation) have posed a new threat to rural archaeology.

Afforestation is one of the most significant of these in terms of its potential impact on archaeological sites. European forestry objectives, as applied to Ireland, have far-reaching consequences across a broad spectrum of interests, including archaeology. One of the underlying difficulties is the general nature of European Union forestry directives which are not tailor-made for individual countries but are designed for the Union as a whole. While the measures may suit a country with a long history in forest management and silviculture, such as France or Germany, they will have a different impact in Ireland.

LEGAL PROTECTION OF ARCHAEOLOGICAL SITES
Protection of archaeology is facilitated under the revised European Union Convention on the Protection of the Archaeological Heritage (1992). This introduced a number of significant requirements for archaeologists and developers, including the preservation, in situ, of archaeological sites where feasible, and the concept that the costs of archaeological mitigation required during development must be borne by the developer.

In response to large-scale developments, the European Union and the Irish Government have introduced new legislation designed to protect, maintain and increase the archaeological record. The European Union is committed to the protection of archaeological heritage. The revised European Convention on the Protection of the Archaeological Heritage (The Valletta Convention), which Ireland ratified in 1997, notes that 'the European archaeological heritage...is seriously threatened with deterioration because of the increasing number of major planning schemes, natural risks, clandestine or unscientific excavations and insufficient public awareness' (Council of Europe 1992). While the previous convention on archaeological protection had been concerned primarily with 'clandestine excavation', the revised convention acknowledges the major threat to archaeological heritage as coming from large-scale construction projects including afforestation (Council of Europe 1993). The convention provides a framework for addressing these threats and for protecting, managing and promoting archaeological heritage within European Member States. As part of that framework, the convention adopted the principle of preservation of sites *in situ*, regarding excavation as a 'last resort' or 'ultimate step' in the search for archaeological information. Parties to the convention are required to involve archaeologists in the planning process of all development schemes, to ensure consultation between archaeologists and planners, and to ensure conservation of archaeological sites found during development *in situ* when feasible (Council of Europe 1992, Article 5). Effectively, it adopted an archaeological policy whereby recording of sites and compiling of inventories is regarded as the minimum requirement for parties to the convention, and archaeological excavation is regarded as exceptional mitigation rather than the norm. A further principle adopted by the convention is that the burden of funding for archaeological requirements during a development scheme should be borne by the developers (*ibid.*, Article 6a).

The most fundamental aspect of the convention is the formal acknowledgement of archaeological heritage as a primary and non-renewable resource that must be conserved for future generations.

National Monuments Acts (1930-1994)
The National Monuments Acts (NMAs) provide legal protection for some archaeological sites.

While signatories to the convention agree to abide by its requirements, most individual Member States have provided additional legal protection to archaeological heritage within their own countries. Legal protection for archaeological sites in Ireland is provided under the National Monuments Acts (NMA), 1930 to 1994. The NMA, 1930, defined a National Monument as:

'a monument or the remains of a monument the preservation of which is a matter of national importance by reason of the historical, architectural, traditional, artistic, or archaeological interest attaching thereto...and the said expression shall be construed as including...the site of the monument and the means of access thereto...'.

National Monuments are legally protected from any unauthorised interference or damage. The term 'monument' was redefined by the 1987 Amendment as:

'any artificial or partly artificial building, structure or erection or group of such buildings, structures or erections, any cave, stone or other natural product...that has been artificially carved, sculptured or worked upon...any, or any part of any, prehistoric or ancient tomb, grave or burial deposit, or ritual, industrial or habitation site, and any place comprising the remains or traces of any such building, structure or erection...'.

As such, 'monuments' are not protected by law but the definition is used to identify sites which require legal protection in the form of 'historic monuments'.

Register of Historic Monuments
The Register of Historic Monuments will, ultimately, list all sites which are considered to be of archaeological significance. The system of notification, however, is a slow process and, at present, the Register only includes about 5,000 sites.

Historic monuments are legally protected by inclusion in the Register of Historic Monuments. An 'historic monument' is defined by the NMA, 1987, as including:

'a prehistoric monument and any monument associated with the commercial, cultural, economic, industrial, military, religious or social history of the place where it is situated or of the country and also includes all monuments in existence before 1700AD or such later date as the Minister may appoint by regulations...' (NMA, 1987, No. 17, Section 1.1).

The Register of Historic Monuments lists known sites and areas which are considered to be of archaeological importance. Under Section 5.10/11 of the 1987 Amendment, it is an offence to 'demolish or remove wholly or in part or disfigure, deface, alter or in any manner interfere with a historic monument that is entered in the Register'. Should a landowner (or occupier) of a Registered monument wish to carry out work 'at or in relation to' a Registered monument, he/she is required to give written notice to the Minister for Arts, Heritage, the Gaeltacht and the Islands.

When a monument is entered into the Register, however, the Minister is required to notify the landowner in writing of the inclusion. To date, the protracted nature of the notification system has limited the number of Registered archaeological sites to about 5,000.

The Record of Monuments and Places
The Record of Monuments and Places is based on previously recorded information and includes all known archaeological and potential archaeological sites.

An interim system of protection was introduced under the 1994 Amendment to the NMA (Section 12.1). The Amendment established the Record of Monuments and Places, which includes 'places where they [the Minister] believe there are monuments' (NMA, 1994, Section 12.1). The Record is based on SMR and Inventory information (see below) and its compilation is the responsibility of the National Monuments and Historic Properties Service. Unlike Registered sites, the owners of land on which a Recorded site exists do not have to be notified of the inclusion of the site in the

Record. The list of sites and accompanying maps are exhibited 'in a prescribed manner in each county' and the onus is on the landowner (or occupier) to be informed of the existence of Recorded sites on their land (*ibid.*, Section 12.2). As with Registered sites, anyone intending to carry out work 'at or in relation to' Recorded sites, must notify the Minister of their intention prior to commencement of such work (*ibid.*, Section 12.3). Contravention of the Act can lead to a maximum fine of £50,000 and/or imprisonment for five years.

Defining Registered and Recorded Monuments
The NMAs define sites for inclusion in the Register and Record. Later archaeological sites are sometimes included, but many lime kilns, for example, were not included in most SMRs and, therefore, will not be afforded legal protection in those counties.

The NMAs define sites for inclusion in the Register of Monuments and the Record of Monuments and Places. The NMHPS has operated a cut-off date of AD 1700, after which sites are not normally considered for inclusion in SMRs and, therefore, are not included in the Register or Record. Post-medieval industrial and vernacular sites are considered by others, however, to be part of the archaeological record (Lambrick 1992; Macinnes and Wickham-Jones 1992b; Rynne 1993), and some have been included in the Record.

The anomaly in the archaeological recording of lime kilns, for example, was clearly demonstrated in the course of this research. Two lime kilns, less than a kilometre apart, but on either side of the Cork/Kerry border, face very different futures. The Cork example (SMR No. CO058-006IA) was meticulously recorded and relocated nearby to allow for road re-alignment (Kelleher 1993). The Kerry example is engulfed by trees within a Coillte plantation (see Appendix 1, no. 1). Coillte operates a policy of not planting on or immediately around monuments listed in the SMR, but the SMR for County Kerry (Stout *et al.* 1990) does not include lime kilns.

The protection of later sites such as lime kilns and other remnants of early industrial activities depends on their inclusion in the record, as was the case with the SMR for Co. Cork (Power *et al.* 1988). The increasing rate of destruction of post-1700AD sites demands that they, at least, be recorded. The inclusion of lime kilns in the Record of Monuments and Places for some counties, eg. Cork and Sligo, is a welcome advance.

THE ARCHAEOLOGICAL SURVEY OF IRELAND
Over the past two decades the NMHPS (formerly OPW) has been conducting a survey of archaeological sites in the country. Three levels are involved: SMR, Inventory, and a detailed archaeological recording of all known monuments.

Identifying and defining an archaeological site in practice can be difficult, requiring extensive research and investigation in the field by experienced field archaeologists. The Archaeological Survey of Ireland, operating for the past two decades under the NMHPS (formerly OPW), progresses through three levels: 1) a paper survey, 2) an inventory field record and 3) a complete field survey of previously recorded sites. In **Level 1**, a database of all known archaeological features in a county is compiled from Ordnance Survey maps, documentary references, aerial photographs (where available) and various other sources. This provides the basis for the SMR. The more advanced **Level 2** 'comprises stage 1 sites plus the results of fieldwork whereby every known site and monument is visited in the field and recorded in sufficient detail' (Power *et al.* 1988, 6). More sites will be added to the SMR at this level. To date, surveys have been completed to Level 1 for all 26 counties in the Republic of Ireland. Level 2 has been compiled for nine Counties with further surveys in progress. The ultimate aspiration of the programme, **Level 3**, is to complete detailed field surveys of all known sites. Completed examples include archaeological surveys of Co. Donegal (Lacy 1983), the Dingle Peninsula (Cuppage 1986), Co. Louth (Buckley and Sweetman 1991) and the Iveragh Peninsula (O'Sullivan and Sheehan 1996).

Sites and Monuments Record (SMR)
An SMR is a list of all known sites of archaeological potential in a county. One of its primary uses is as a reference database for county planning committees and for State/EU-assisted planting proposals. (Applications for planting are checked against the SMR map by the Forest Service.) There is often, however, a tendency to over rely on SMRs at the expense of unrecorded sites.

Archaeological sites and monuments which are have been identified to date, or are known to have existed, are included in the SMR for the county in which they occur. These records have been compiled over the past sixteen years through a comprehensive, countrywide survey. SMRs are preliminary listings of known archaeological features in a county, and they act as the basis for incorporating the results of the Archaeological Survey of Ireland into the Record of Monuments and Places. Although SMRs are non-statutory lists, they play a central role in the protection of sites in forestry and are used by the Forest Service for assessing an area to be planted. Most published SMRs were largely based on the Level 1 paper survey and inevitably included sites which will eventually be identified as non-archaeological in nature. These sites are identified at Inventory level and excluded from the Record of Monuments and Places.

Ordnance Survey six-inch maps, compiled between 1824 and 1940, are the main cartographic source of information since they depict archaeological sites that were known at the time, many of which are now destroyed. Ringforts, megalithic tombs, earthen mounds, *fulachta fiadh*, lime kilns and holy wells are some of the most common site-types represented. In some areas the cartographic detail is extensive and the six-inch maps, in particular, include a high proportion of sites. In other areas, and for different site-types, the representation is extremely low. In parts of counties Galway, Leitrim and Mayo, for example, as few as five percent of known sites were marked on Ordnance Survey six-inch maps (Cooney 1993, 16).

Many of the site classifications included in SMRs (for example, circular enclosures) are descriptive rather than interpretative since they are classified on the basis of cartographic depiction or general documentary evidence. While in reality one circular enclosure might be a nineteenth-century tree ring, another might be a ringfort or a cashel, and yet others might be natural or non-archaeological features. The SMR is therefore a preliminary record of known and possible archaeological sites in a county and cannot be used as a definitive list of archaeology in any area of any county.

A published SMR consists of a listing of all recorded archaeological sites in the county accompanied by corresponding maps with the sites clearly marked on them. SMRs have been distributed to most local and semi-State bodies, as well as local interest groups such as historical and archaeological groups. The maps are available for public consultation at most county libraries and corporation offices and are now regarded as essential elements in local planning and development procedures.

Inventory surveys
Sites included in an SMR are inspected in the field to provide additional information for Inventory surveys. The published Inventory includes more detail on the nature, location and condition of archaeological sites. Some of the Inventory databases detail the type of land use around a monument; this information

The second level (Level 2) of the Archaeological Survey is represented by Inventory Surveys which build upon the information gathered in the SMRs. Sites are located, briefly surveyed and photographed and then entered into a standard data base which is finally published as an inventory. Inventories give brief details of each site: type, dimension, location, siting and condition. To date, 17 counties have been, or are in the process of being surveyed at this level. While inventory surveying involves field visits during which many previously unrecorded sites have been discovered, its brief is to record known sites only and not to actively search for new sites.

*could be used as a basis for
assessing the impact of
afforestation on archaeological
sites and for identifying sites in
existing forestry that require
remedial action or
management.*

Where inventory descriptions indicate the type of land in which a site occurs, or the land use of an area, it is possible to compile a preliminary list of sites in forestry. Although land use is not noted in many of the inventories, those for Co. Cork give a brief indication of the land use in and around each site. During the course of this present research, an examination of the archaeological inventories for West Cork (Power 1992) and Mid Cork (Power 1997), identified almost 200 sites and monuments as being planted and/or in forestry at the time of inspection (see Appendix 2). Much of the fieldwork for the inventories, however, was carried out in the early/mid 1980s before the current widespread afforestation programme. The list, therefore is not definitive. Nonetheless, it provides a basis from which an assessment of sites in existing forestry could be made. Many of the sites in forestry were inaccessible at the time of carrying out the surveys and therefore have not been confirmed as existing. Others have already been damaged or are in danger of being damaged because of their close proximity to the trees. This information could be used to assess the potential impact of afforestation on sites in forestry.

***Preliminary status of the
archaeological surveys***
*The Archaeological Surveys
only represent known sites and
monuments. Vast areas of the
countryside have never been
investigated, and many
monuments and sites remain
undiscovered. The possibility
of their existence must be
considered in all forestry
developments.*

The SMRs and Inventory Surveys represent the most comprehensive census of archaeological sites ever compiled in Ireland. It cannot be overemphasised, however, that they only account for recorded sites and that many more remain to be discovered. Many of the sites listed were originally identified by early Ordnance Survey cartographers who rarely ventured into unenclosed, marginal and upland areas. As a result, there are considerable areas of the countryside which have never been surveyed and which probably contain thousands of unrecorded archaeological sites. Since publication of the SMR for Co. Cork (Power *et al.* 1988), for example, an estimated 5,000 additional monuments have been discovered in the county (Cork Archaeological Survey, pers. comm.). This gives some indication of the number of relatively high-visibility sites which exist, unrecorded, throughout the country. Since these sites were not previously recorded, there would have been no mechanism in place to protect them from developments such as afforestation.

The nature of archaeological remains is such that the majority of sites included in an SMR will be upstanding stone or earthen monuments (Fig. 5). They therefore represent a limited selection of site-types which will give a bias to the apparent representation of certain periods in prehistory and later periods. Early prehistoric settlement sites, for example, exist throughout the country but their low visibility makes them extremely difficult to locate. They are, therefore, under-represented in all SMRs and Inventories.

To view SMRs as definitive listings of archaeological sites in Ireland is to grossly misinterpret their function. SMRs were compiled as the first stage in an on-going attempt to identify and ultimately protect sites. They collate the sites known at the time of publication and must be updated frequently to include newly identified sites. It is essential, therefore, that before any large-scale development in a relatively unexplored landscape takes place, the area should be assessed by suitably experienced archaeologists for its archaeological potential. At present, there are no specific requirements for archaeological surveying other than those included under Environmental Impact Assessments and/or Local Authority planning regulations for the forest industry.

Fig. 5. *The hillfort at Spinans Hill, Co. Wicklow. Forestry has been allowed to intrude to the rampart of the site (John Scarry, Dúchas).*

PRE-AFFORESTATION ARCHAEOLOGICAL IMPACT ASSESSMENT
At present, the only form of pre-afforestation field assessment is through the EIA process. An EIA is required for planting over 70 hectares of land. Archaeological impact assessments need to be carried out in a professional and comprehensive manner. Assessments that are based on SMR information are not adequate to prevent damage to archaeological sites in the development area. Field assessment (see below) is the more basic criteria for an archaeological impact assessment. The use of more sophisticated site-detection tools must also be considered. The record, to date, suggests that the standard of pre-afforestation impact assessments has been, at the very least, questionable.

Afforestation and industrial developments in rural areas are probably the most visible indicators of change in rural land-use, but land reclamation and enclosure of commonage also have potential impacts on archaeology. Of these, only industrial developments are fully regulated to minimise their impact on archaeology, the environment and on the local communities. Planning permission is required for the construction of industrial sites and many will require an Environmental Impact Assessment (EIA) before construction. Each aspect of their potential impact on the environment, wildlife and archaeology is considered within the EIA. While there are often complex difficulties involved, the majority are resolved through regulations and, in the case of archaeological sites, either protection or excavation, at the developer's expense.

There is a lingering assumption that agriculture is not as intrusive or as damaging to its surroundings as industrial activities but as agriculture becomes more intensive and introduces new aspects such as forestry, the issue deserves reconsideration.

Until recently, up to 200 hectares of land could be planted without archaeological assessment. This threshold was reduced to a compromise figure of 70 hectares after protracted debate between the D/AFF and the D/OE; the latter had proposed a threshold reportedly as low as 25 hectares (Scanlan 1995, 46). Afforestation over 70 hectares is now subjected to planning regulations in the form of an EIA, under European Communities (Environmental Impact Assessment) Regulations, 1996 (SI No. 101 of 1996). In addition, a new provision regarding incremental or add-on forestry was introduced. Aggregate afforestation within a three-year period over 70 hectares in size will also require an EIA. Previously, it was possible for a landowner to plant contiguous blocks of land up to 199 hectares each without impact assessment (Fig. 6).

Fig. 6. *The Glenmalure valley in Co. Wicklow is being progressively engulfed by forestry. As this is a prime area for prehistoric settlement, field assessment should take place before any further forestry is planted (Aerofilms).*

While the new threshold of 70 hectares is a significant reduction in terms of the environment and landscape, its benefits for archaeology are likely to be limited. The reduction will, however, bring some of the larger developments into the assessment process and there will be an increase in the number of archaeological surveys carried out pre-planting. These surveys must be carried out in a competent, professional and appropriate manner, which previous research (e.g. Byrnes 1992) suggests has not always been the case. Byrnes (*ibid.*, 114) reported that over a period of 16 months only seven EIAs were submitted for forest developments, six of which were semi-State proposals. The study considered aspects of the EIA process which, either directly or by reference, involved archaeological considerations. One of the principal concerns was that there was no available information on the details of the archaeological 'surveys' carried out. There were suggestions in other cases that the so-called 'survey' involved little more than consultation of the SMR for the region (*ibid.*, 20). Byrnes also noted a difficulty in identifying the archaeologists involved in carrying out the EIAs, noting that the name and qualification was recorded in only one case. Likewise, the methodology used in carrying out the surveys was only stated in one case.

The EIA for afforestation in Coomacheo (Ballyvourney) Co. Cork, for example, allocates two sentences to archaeology:

> *'Following a full field survey and examination of manuscripts, there is no evidence to indicate the presence of any archaeological site, monument or structure on the lands designated for this project. If any remains are uncovered during forest operations they will be carefully marked and left undisturbed.'* (Coillte Teoranta 1992a, 41, sect. 4.9).

The 'project' involved 287 hectares of land consisting mainly of blanket peat, partially cut-over and ranging in depth from 0.5m to over 3m, with the Clydagh River flowing through the area (*ibid.*, 15). The nature of the terrain was such that some archaeological remains would normally be expected and it is perhaps surprising that not a single monument (pre-bog walls, toghers and other organic remains, standing stones, megalithic tombs, artefacts, etc.) was recorded. In the absence of an archaeological report, however, it is impossible to interpret what a 'full field survey and examination of manuscripts' entailed.

It is essential that standards are introduced to govern the procedures followed, the qualifications and field experience of the archaeologist involved, and the publication of the results. A proposed procedure for carrying out the archaeological component of an EIA, as suggested by Condit (1991), is summarised as follows:

Development Plans:	Earthmoving; Excavations; Foundation trenches; Pipe-laying; Road building, Quarrying; Planting; Landscaping.
Archaeological Study:	Field inspection; Documentary research; Aerial photographic survey; Local traditions/folklore; Sites and Monuments Records; National Museum records.
Further Investigation:	Test excavation; Resistivity Survey; Magnetometer survey.

The above procedures will result in a statement of the archaeological impact and recommendations on how the impact can be minimised, for example, through avoidance, monitoring of the development, full-scale excavation, etc. The Irish Association of Professional Archaeologists (IAPA) has compiled a referral list of archaeologists available to carry out such survey work, which will afford some degree of standardisation. The National Monuments Acts (1930-1994) require all archaeological excavation to be licensed; in addition, the NMHPS now requires monitoring of large-scale developments to be licensed and recommends that all archaeological monitoring should be licensed (Heritage Service 1997, 4). Therefore, where an EIA recommends archaeological monitoring of planting preparation, the procedure will be overseen by the NMHPS and the NMI.

Local authorities
Local authorities have an increasingly important role in the protection of archaeological sites. They now have an opportunity to exercise a degree of control

Local authorities have an increasingly significant role to play in the protection of archaeology in their regions. This is reflected by the number of archaeologists currently working for or in consultation with the authorities. The introduction of amendments to the Local Government planning

over afforestation particularly in sensitive areas. Local authorities will be notified of all planting in their area over 25 hectares. They have also been asked to designate areas sensitive to afforestation. Once designated, the Forest Service will notify the authority of all proposals to plant in the area. The benefits of these recently introduced regulations will require further investigation and review.

regulations clearly defines the potential for that role. The lowering of the threshold at which an EIA is required and the regulations regarding incremental afforestation will have the immediate effect of providing a greater degree of archaeological assessment for large-scale afforestation. Considering that the majority of plantations are under 30 hectares in size, however, their most positive effects are likely to be related to the local environment rather than to the archaeology of an area.

In recognition of the limitations, the D/OE introduced a number of useful, although non-statutory, procedures. A system of notification to local authorities of all grant-assisted afforestation over 25 hectares has applied since 1996. The local authority has a month in which to comment on these proposals and any observations submitted to the Forest Service during that period will be taken into account in the processing of the application. Where archaeologists are consulted by local authorities, this system should provide additional protection for recorded sites and areas where unrecorded archaeological sites might be expected to occur. The effectiveness of the amendments will be reviewed by Government in 1999.

A second equally important, again non-statutory, introduction is the 'Designation of Areas Sensitive to Afforestation' procedure. Local authorities have been invited to designate such areas with respect to a range of criteria including 'protection of natural and archaeological heritage'. The local authority provides the Forest Service with a map of their designated areas and in return the Forest Service will notify the authority of all applications to plant in the designated area regardless of size. Again, the authority has a month in which to make observations regarding the appropriate nature of the proposed planting.

These are progressive approaches which have the potential to act as co-ordinating systems for interaction between archaeologists, local authorities, and the Forest Service. Where local authorities do not consult archaeologists, however, it is not known what benefits, if any, can be acquired for the protection of sites in forestry. The efficiency and success of the procedures will require further investigation and a review of their practical implications for archaeology.

ARCHAEOLOGICAL FIELD SURVEYS AND ASSESSMENTS

There are many unrecorded archaeological sites in Ireland. Some exist in remote areas that have not yet been surveyed, while many others remain below ground. Different factors can sometimes be used to predict where particular types of sites are likely to occur. In general, however, field-work is an essential part of the identification process. The most basic ground-level surveying is site inspection of known archaeological monuments. Field surveying is also carried out to identify indicators of previously unrecorded sites. Both forms of field work are associated with pre-development archaeological impact assessment. The use of aerial photography, and geophysical

Predicting where archaeological sites are likely to occur is fraught with difficulties, although trends can sometimes be identified. Factors such as a nearby freshwater source, the availability of raw materials, sheltered and dry land away from flood plains, the presence of upstanding monuments, etc., can suggest the possible locations of settlement sites. Changes in the landscape, however, can mask prehistoric sites and the indicators might not always be evident without detailed surveying. Prehistoric water sources may dry up, favourable lakeside sites be covered by raised bog as at Boora Bog (Ryan 1980), upland sites be obscured by blanket bog. The source of raw material may not be obvious or may have been exhausted. Other factors, such as an association between site locations, have been used as predictive models for prehistoric activity. Megalithic tombs, for example, point to the existence of nearby sites since they tend to be closely associated with centres of human settlement (Grogan 1991, 59; Mount 1996).

Field-based surveys and investigations are carried out for two main reasons: for research purposes (see, for example, Zvelebil *et al.* 1987, Anderson 1993) or for monitoring of developments that are likely to have an impact

and geochemical surveying techniques, can increase the possibility of detecting low-visibility sites in particular. In exceptional cases, archaeological excavation will be required to define the nature and extent of the site.

on archaeological sites (for example, Cleary *et al.* 1987; Keeley 1996). The former are normally designed to explore a particular aspect of archaeology, or as is the case with the National Monuments Survey, to compile information on sites and monuments.

The importance of field assessment and survey work is also demonstrated by the Limerick SMR; over 64% of standing stones included in the SMR were discovered by field survey (Kirwan 1993, 143). Similarly, 40% of the 25 known *fulachta fiadh* were discovered either by field survey or by accident (five were discovered after ploughing for afforestation) (*ibid.*, 144).

In its most basic forms, fieldwork consists of inspecting and briefly recording a monument, or walking over an area looking for archaeological indicators such as artefacts. Site inspection prior to development and subsequent monitoring of construction is essential for identifying and protecting archaeological sites. The information can then be used to advise the developer of any precautions required to prevent damage to the site. Even where a site has been included in the Inventory-level survey, it may sometimes be necessary to re-inspect it prior to development. The Inventory records the condition of sites at the time of inspection; in many cases this is already ten or more years ago.

After initial site inspection, remedial action may be necessary to protect the site from the development. Where the site boundary is not obvious, as will sometimes be the case with earthen monuments, for example, it will need to be defined by the archaeologist and a clear form of staking may be necessary to distinguish the site. In some cases, the use of sophisticated detection methods may be warranted, particularly where indications of an archaeological site exist but are not sufficiently obvious to define and record the extent of the site. Concentrations of flint artefacts, for example, indicate the presence of a prehistoric site, but further investigation will often be necessary to determine the nature and exact location of the sites. Occasionally, when other methods of site-detection and recording fail to define a site, pre-development excavation may be necessary. Although the Forest Service guidelines on archaeology allow for the possibility of excavation, as far as could be ascertained, there has been no instance of an excavation pre-afforestation in Ireland to date.

Promoting awareness of archaeology
The presence of archaeologists in the field also serves as a form of promotion and awareness of archaeological heritage.

An indirect but important effect of field surveying is the interaction that it provides between professional archaeologists and the public. O'Sullivan and Sheehan (1993, 147) comment that the activities of the South-West Kerry Archaeological Field Survey encouraged 'a broad spectrum of people — in particular landowners and survey trainees — to become aware of and interested in archaeological heritage'. Similarly, Power (1993, 138) notes that the presence of professional field surveys has coincided with a revival in local historical and archaeological groups.

In addition, many previously unrecorded sites have been identified by local 'amateurs' whose interest in archaeology was prompted by the activities of archaeological surveys in their areas. Ultimately, the protection of archaeological sites relies on the level of awareness of archaeology at local levels.

Site-detection methods
A variety of techniques exist that can be used to detect or define archaeological sites.

Once an area of prehistoric activity has been identified, scientific detection methods and excavation can be employed to provide further information. The approach taken will depend on the type of land (soil, location), the land-use, and the size of the area involved. Given that forestry has moved onto a wide range of soil and land types, an equally wide range of field surveying techniques must be considered in response. In blanket bogland, for example, archaeological sites lie hidden under peat and will not be detected without the use of probes or by exposure during excavation of drainage trenches, etc. (Fig. 7). In marginal areas or in degraded bogland, field walking alone might produce positive results, with archaeological features visible at ground level. The use of probing as a method of site detection in blanket bogland has produced extensive results in the past, e.g. the Céide Fields, Co. Mayo (Caulfield 1983). While it has been described as 'unfashionable', English Heritage (David 1995, 28) argues that it 'should perhaps not be so easily dismissed'.

Fig. 7. *Prospection before planting on blanket bog, as here at Aghavannagh, Co. Wicklow, has the potential to reveal archaeology (Bord Fáilte).*

Aerial photography
Aerial photographs can be used to identify previously unrecorded sites. As with all methods of archaeological surveying, there are limiting factors to its use. These include land-use, land-type, weather conditions, costs, etc. Where appropriate, however, it is a valuable site-detection tool. An aerial perspective can also place sites in a broader landscape context, identifying large-scale monuments and features associated with previously recorded sites. Adequate aerial coverage exists for some regions, but the possibility of commissioning

As techniques of analysis improve, increasing numbers of sites can now be identified from aerial photographs. The use of stereoscopic equipment can enhance a vertical aerial photograph to give a three-dimensional view of the countryside, enhancing features that are not visible at ground level. In many cases, sites identified from aerial photographs, especially through crop, soil and grass marks, may be impossible to identify on the ground without the use of geophysical techniques. These sites are potentially as significant as their upstanding counterparts.

In 1986, UCC and OPW undertook an assessment of the value of using medium altitude (1:10,000), vertical, stereo photographs for recording archaeological sites (Doody 1993, 99). The study area was mostly under pasture and therefore good preservation of sites was expected. The results of the study demonstrated the usefulness of aerial photography — in

aerial reconnaissance for large-scale developments must be considered. A re-examination of adequate existing photographs will often identify previously unrecorded sites.

some areas there was a 100% increase in the number of sites recorded (*ibid.*).

The most commonly discovered sites using aerial photography are of earth and stone, either upstanding or subterranean. Aerial photographic reconnaissance will often place previously recorded sites in a broader landscape context (Figs. 8 and 9). Extra-mural features around earthworks, for example, are frequently only identified from the air. Similarly, the extensive nature of hillforts and field systems may be difficult to define at ground level but can be recorded with relative ease from aerial photographs.

The main aerial photographic coverage for Ireland comes from the Geological Survey of Ireland (GSI) whose high-altitude (1:30,000) vertical photographs of the country were taken between 1973 and 1977. These photographs are generally only useful for identifying larger sites such as earthworks and low-relief sites (Condit 1997, 46). To identify smaller sites, such as ring-barrows, aerial photographs at low (1:5,000) and medium (1:10,000) altitudes have to be used. A range of aerial photographs was used in the compilation of some of the Sites and Monuments Records and produced a considerable number of previously unidentified sites. In Co. Limerick, for example, 65% of ring-barrows included in the SMR were identified from aerial photographs, compared with 3.7% represented on Ordnance Survey six-inch maps, and the remainder identified through fieldwork (Kirwan 1993, 142) .

Fig. 8. *Prehistoric earthworks occur as cropmarks in this aerial photograph taken near Carlow town (Tom Condit).*

In recent years, aerial reconnaissance and photography have played significant parts in archaeological surveys, for example, the Cork-Dublin gas pipeline (Cleary *et al.* 1987), the Cork Archaeological Survey (Power 1993), the Iveragh Peninsula Survey (O'Sullivan and Sheehan 1996), and the work of the Discovery Programme (for example, Grogan *et al.* 1995). Newly commissioned photographs, at lower levels than the GSIs, have been taken specifically for these and other archaeological projects. In all cases, the analysis of the aerial photographs produced previously unrecorded sites.

The value of aerial coverage is demonstrated, for example, by the work of the Cork Archaeological Survey; the exceptionally dry conditions during the summer of 1989 emphasised soil and crop marks, resulting in the discovery of 200 enclosures and earthworks (Power 1993, 139).

Fig. 9. *A complex of earthworks occur as cropmarks in this aerial photograph taken at Fenniscourt, Co. Carlow (Ordnance Survey).*

Aerial photography has, however, inherent limitations which must be understood if it is to be used effectively. Very low relief sites in pasture, particularly if unimproved, can be photographed effectively as shadow sites, but need slanting light, haze-free conditions and reasonably short grass. Soil marks need freshly ploughed soil without surface drying. Parch- or cropmarks, particularly in cereal crops, reveal many sites but optimum conditions occur very rarely in most parts of the country and may last only days. Parch marks in grass occur more frequently. Green crops such as sugar beet or heavy vegetation usually preclude good results. In areas of thick blanket (or raised) bog, cropmarks do not obtain and peat has usually grown up over low-relief sites. However, features exposed in cut-over or degraded bog may show well in low-light condition. Ultimately, aerial photography is a complementary tool and not a replacement for field work. In most cases, a follow-up field visit on the ground will be required to fully assess the nature of the site. These are, however, factors which can be taken into consideration in pre-development plans.

Where large areas of land are likely to be afforested, aerial photographs and reconnaissance may be an invaluable surveying tool, particularly in remote areas which are difficult to survey at ground level. Medium and low-level photographs are available for some regions, but in many it will be necessary to commission new surveys. While aerial photography can be expensive, the costs could be kept to a minimum especially where large areas are likely to be afforested by forestry companies, co-operatives, etc. Previous studies demonstrate how an area can be covered relatively quickly, thereby keeping costs to a minimum. The area between Fermoy and Mallow, along the Blackwater Valley (*c.* 20 miles x 5 miles), for example, was covered in six hours of flying and resulted in the discovery (albeit in exceptional weather conditions) of over 200 previously unrecorded sites (*ibid.*).

In other cases, adequate photographs will already exist and should be analysed before development begins. Given the continuing advancement of analytical techniques for studying aerial photographs, reassessment of existing photographs may prove to be very successful. Kelleher (1995) reported a high success rate in identifying previously unrecorded sites through the use of computer enhancement and mapping programmes to analyse aerial photographs. The results were particularly impressive in identifying field systems and associated enclosures in marginal areas. The study employed the Bradford Air-Photographic Rectification System and MORPH (a programme designed for studying morphological aspects of the landscape from aerial photographs) — programmes extensively used in the Britain for identifying and mapping archaeological sites (Kelleher, pers. comm.).

Geophysical and geochemical analysis
Where appropriate, geophysical and geochemical analyses can identify and/or define areas of archaeological significance. Their potential for identifying sites pre-afforestation must be considered.

Geophysical and geochemical survey techniques are relatively recent and developing forms of archaeological site prospecting. As with all forms of surveying, the techniques (e.g. magnetometer, electromagnetic and magnetic susceptibility surveys and phosphate analysis) are only applied in appropriate landscapes. Variations in land-use, geology, soil types, etc., and the size of the area under assessment, will determine the suitability of employing geophysical and/or geochemical surveys. These are specialised techniques of analysis that require trained and experienced personnel to carry out the survey. They are generally useful for identifying sub-soil traces of human activity in the form of buried earth and stone features, including levelled stone walls, pits and areas of burning that might be associated with human activity, etc. These features are identified through anomalies in the instrument readings that can be interpreted by an experienced surveyor to distinguish between natural and human causes. The techniques, however, are limited in their application. It is not yet possible, for example, to detect organic structures (e.g. toghers) in deep organic sediments, although such features might be detected on the margins of wetlands or in islands of relatively dry land within wetlands (David 1995, 12). Magnetometer surveying, for example, is most suited to identifying features closer to ground level, although it can, in certain conditions, identify anomalies up to one metre below ground level. On appropriate land, a detailed magnetometer survey can identify features as small as post-holes (*ibid.*).

The use of geochemical and geophysical surveying techniques will have to be considered in pre-afforestation assessment, to detect sites in areas of high archaeological potential, and to clarify the nature and extent of sites whose boundaries cannot be defined by other, non-destructive, means.

MONITORING OF PLANTING PREPARATION
Many archaeological sites will only become apparent when the ground is disturbed. The presence of experienced field archaeologists during invasive planting preparation is necessary to identify features of archaeological significance.

It is not always possible to detect archaeological sites prior to development. Some sites will only be identified when the ground is disturbed. Ploughing or digging of trenches for mound-planting or for drainage can expose traces of previously unidentified sites in the form of artefact scatters and features such as buried earth and stone structures, hearths, post-holes, timber trackways, etc. Although the use of heavy machinery often makes identification difficult, an experienced field archaeologist will notice such features when they are exposed.

In recent years monitoring of invasive developments has become more common in Ireland. Large-scale projects such as the construction of major roads and gas pipelines now require archaeological assessment pre-development, and monitoring during the construction phase. Many significant archaeological sites have been identified during this process. Monitoring of road construction in Co. Laois, for example, identified an extensive Iron Age complex of ring ditches, associated features and artefacts (Keeley 1996). Similarly, there were no surface traces of the cluster of Later Bronze Age houses and associated structures at Curraghatoor, Co. Tipperary (Doody 1987, 36); the site was recognised when patches of burnt soil were noticed during monitoring of top-soil removal for the construction of a gas pipeline (Cleary *et al.* 1987). Without the attendance of archaeologists, it is likely that such sites would not have been identified and that they would have been destroyed by construction work.

CHAPTER 2

Forestry in Ireland

While there is debate about the extent to which Ireland was forested in prehistory, there is no doubt that woodlands were once extensive and varied. Native mixed forests incorporated a range of species, such as oak, elm, Scots pine and ash on the better soils, and hazel, birch and alder on the poorer soils. The survival of native tree species varied across the country. Scots pine, for example, probably disappeared in most places in the early centuries of the Christian era but survived in the Killarney region until about 1,300 years ago (Mitchell and Ryan 1996, 111). Where Ireland was once heavily wooded we now have extensive pasture land, bogland and thin mountain soils. Disease and climatic changes contributed to woodland demise, but the impact of human activity is far more significant and more evident (Mitchell 1976; Neeson 1991 and O'Carroll 1984). Early prehistoric clearance of trees ranged from small-scale clearing in the early Neolithic to relatively large-scale felling in the Bronze Age. As agriculture developed, large areas of forests were burnt or cut down and the land grazed or planted with crops. Throughout the medieval period Irish woodlands were increasingly exploited for practical, political and economic purposes. During the sixteenth and early seventeenth centuries, the tree cover of Ireland was finally decimated by a wave of extensive felling for timber export.

The only semi-natural, native stands are now confined to small pockets, the largest of which forms part of the Killarney National Park (Office of Public Works 1990). They constitute only a tiny fraction of the total tree cover in Ireland and survive mostly on the acid soils of sandstone and granite in the mountains of Kerry, Wicklow, Connemara and Donegal (de Buitléar 1995, 111). Most of these are now protected by law and managed as important heritage and amenity areas.

Ireland has a poor record of woodland management stretching back long before the clearances of the sixteenth century (see Neeson 1991 for a comprehensive history). Prior to the early 1900s, there were no formal management systems in place (with a few exceptions on the larger estates) and trees grew as wild and natural or semi-natural woodlands.

The lack of an historical silviculture in Ireland, coupled with the small size of Irish farms, has had significant consequences for Irish forestry which are manifested in attitudes and in practice. The notion of actually planting land (regardless of quality) has always been an anathema to Irish farmers and trees have been generally regarded as useful for little more than shelter or as a source of fuel.

A forest plantation, coniferous or deciduous, requires a varying degree of management if it is to be maintained successfully. Forest management involves site and seed choice, ground preparation and drainage, vegetation control, thinning, pruning and, in the case of commercial plantations, extraction. At its latest stage, it incorporates a range of techniques from skilled hand-felling to large-scale clear-felling. Modern forest management is not confined to the welfare of the trees themselves but is also concerned with the relationship between the forest and issues such as the environment, public access and appreciation, local water sources, ecology and heritage features. Sophisticated management programmes are now in place in most of the National Parks and Nature Reserves as well as in some of the commercial forest plantations.

While the public is aware of the environmental and ecological benefits of deciduous woodlands, there is a general dislike and scepticism about commercial and coniferous plantations, in particular. There are, however, some progressive policies in place which are designed to develop forestry as a profitable industry while trying to accommodate environmental, ecological, agricultural, community and archaeological concerns.

State forestry
Government involvement in forestry has varied from low-key planting programmes in the past to the current promotion on a large scale.

In the early decades of this century just over one percent of Irish land was under trees and less than eight percent of that was State owned (Neeson 1991, 110). Various governments attempted to improve the situation but it was not until 1958 that a substantial annual planting target of 10,000 hectares (24,700 acres) was established. While this target was not achieved until the late 1960s, it initiated the development of State forestry and research into forestry in Ireland. A sustained programme since then has increased the annual planting target to 30,000 hectares (semi-State and private planting) and has increased the overall forest cover to about eight percent, despite the decline of State planting in recent years.

Forestry is the most travelled sector within Government Departments. Responsibility for forestry has shifted from the Department of Lands to the Department of Fisheries and Forestry (later the Department of Fisheries, Forestry and Tourism), to the Department of Energy, on to the Department of Agriculture, Food and Forestry and, most recently, to the Department of the Marine and Natural Resources. Regardless of its position, modern Irish forest policy is strongly influenced by external factors, particularly European Union regulations, directives and financial assistance. Until recently, however, the practical development of forestry was curtailed by traditional agricultural practices and land use.

One of the limiting factors in acquiring land for afforestation has always been the scarcity of suitable and affordable land. As a consequence of prohibitive land prices, in particular, the State was often forced to acquire land which was limited in its yield potential. During the 1950s, the Forest Service was involved in the development of low ground-pressure tractor units and large heavy-duty ploughs which allowed planting of blanket peatland (Farrell and Boyle 1990, 70). The most innovatory development was the tunnel plough, first introduced in Glenamoy, Co. Mayo, which allowed planting of the hardier tree species on deep peat soils. With Sitka spruce, for example, tunnel ploughing will allow the roots to extend 80cm or more into the soil, improving wind resistance and allowing unrestricted lateral rooting. Blanket peatland was regarded as ideal territory for the expansion of forestry, particularly because of its low agricultural value. The influential Cameron Report (FAO 1951) also encouraged planting of western peatlands on the grounds that it would 'provide a great increase in attractiveness to tourists for large sections of Western Ireland by improving considerably the scenic and sporting amenities' (Farrell and Boyle 1990, 71). Planting on blanket bogland rapidly became commonplace, peaking in the mid 1980s with approximately 170,000 hectares of intact blanket bogland afforested (Hickie 1990, 7).

In more recent years, Coillte Teoranta has moved away from planting on undamaged bogland, partially because of the relatively limited economic returns but also in response to pressure from environmental concerns.

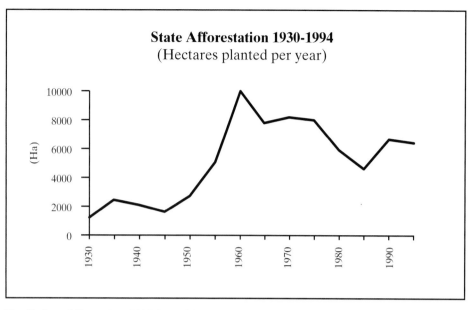

Fig. 10. *State Afforestation (1930-94). While State planting reached a peak in the 1960s, it has since been overtaken by private planting rates (See Fig. 13).*

International concerns
Concern for the environment is at an all time high, particularly with regard to the destruction of tree cover. The European Union is committed to increasing woodland cover to help reduce the strain on tropical rain forests.

The current promotion of forestry in Ireland is largely a result of a world-wide drive to reduce the stress on tropical rain forests (Anon. (a) 1995, 7). Concern about their destruction reached an unprecedented level in 1992 with the United Nations' conference on the environment and development in Brazil (The Earth Summit), which produced a world-level political agreement on forests. While tropical rain forests were the main concern, the 'Statement of Principles' agreed at the conference acknowledged the importance of all forests to the global environment. The European Union is part of the agreement to improve environmental conditions world-wide and the subsequent promotion of European forestry has resulted in restructuring of Irish strategies on forestry.

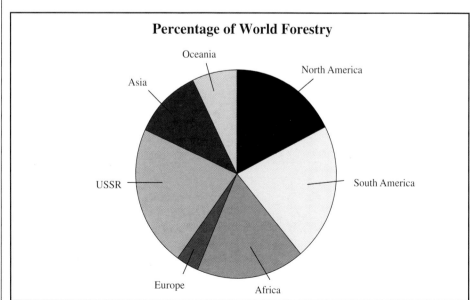

Fig. 11. *Distribution of World Forestry. Europe, with only 3.7% of the world's forests, imports more timber than any of the other continents.*

EUROPE
The European Union is the world's largest importer of timber. It has programmes which are specifically designed to increase internal production of timber both for environmental and for economic reasons. European Union regulations and directives have shaped Irish forest policy.

While Ireland can never grow enough trees to directly influence the global environment, it is committed to the overall agreement to increase European self-sufficiency in timber, thereby reducing the pressure on rain forests and the knock-on effects of their destruction. Europe imports more timber each year than any other continent and the demand for natural wood and timber products has never been higher. While the economic benefits of increasing Irish timber production are obvious, there is also greater public awareness of the significance of trees in local and national terms. In tourism, health issues and the expanding commercial timber industry, the potential benefits of well-planned planting programmes have yet to be fully realised. The leisure industry, for example, has only begun to explore the potential for woodlands in Ireland as a source of tourist and recreational activities.

Until recently, more pressing concerns largely overshadowed the forest industry in Europe. European Union forests cover about 25% of the land, a figure which had been declining through neglect, exploitation, disease and fire (*ibid.*, 5). Since 1992, however, considerable attention has been focused on the subject and forestry is now considered to be a major growth industry, especially in countries which are currently lacking in woodland cover. Ireland is an obvious country for expansion of the industry.

Percentage of land under forestry (European Union)
Ireland has less than 8% of the land under forestry — the lowest percentage in the European Union, which has an average of 31%.

Percentage of Land Under Forestry (EU)
(Source: D/AFF 1996, 7)

Ireland	8
Netherlands	9
United Kingdom	10
Denmark	10
Belgium	22
Spain	27
Italy	29
France	30
Germany	30
Luxembourg	34
Portugal	35
Greece	44
Austria	46
Sweden	62
Finland	69
European Average	**31**

Ireland has the lowest percentage (8%) of land under forestry in the Europe Union. The average is about 31%. It has been recognised for many years that our mild, damp climate is ideal for rapid tree growth, with growth potential in some areas amongst the highest in Europe (Dunstan 1985, 93). While Ireland has an exceptional opportunity to increase woodland cover, it has an equally important obligation to respect rural communities, agriculture, wildlife, the environment and, of primary concern here, archaeology.

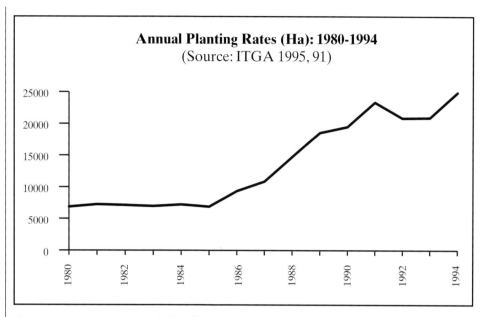

Annual Planting Rates (Ha): 1980-1994
(Source: ITGA 1995, 91)

Fig. 12. *Annual Planting Rates (1980-1994). Annual planting targets have set a general trend upwards since the mid-1980s.*

European forestry directives
The sectors targeted for grant assistance change depending on European and world markets.

It is widely acknowledged that the level of tree planting is strongly determined by the availability of European Union grants — the more attractive the grants, the more trees are planted. Furthermore, the level and structure of the grant-aid has a significant effect on the type of land planted. Planting grants were first introduced under the 'Western Package' in 1981, which targeted farmers in the western counties regarded as working in disadvantaged areas in marginal agricultural land (Mulloy 1991, 343). The scheme largely failed to entice farmers into forestry and it was not until the structure of the grant schemes was adjusted in the early 1990s that forestry became an attractive alternative for farmers. Since then, further restructuring and redistribution of agricultural funds have led to a widespread uptake of forestry grants throughout the country.

In 1988, the European Community Commission published a policy document dealing specifically with European Union objectives for forestry (Anon. 1988). One of the main objectives of the strategy was to promote forestry as an alternative form of land use in an attempt to reduce the current surplus of traditional agricultural products. At that time, sheep grazing was the main form of agriculture in the disadvantaged and marginal zones and was heavily subsidised by the Ewe Premium Scheme. There was, therefore, no immediate advantage to switching from sheep to forestry since grants for the two existed in competition with each other. As a result, most of the planting in uplands and marginal areas was carried out by the State and can be seen today as maturing forests throughout the country.

European forest investment is carried out under the Accompanying Measures of the Common Agricultural Policy Reform and the Structural Funds of the European Union. As part of those schemes, financial assistance is available for afforestation, woodland regeneration and improvement, forest roads, harvesting, technical assistance and back-up measures. The level of funding has risen significantly over the past five years to an all-time high in 1994, when a total of £22.4 million in grant-aid was paid out for planting and maintaining commercial crops. Compared with the total for 1992 (£9.4 million), the increase reflects the emphasis placed on forestry since then. While European Union financial assistance is committed only to the end of 1997, there is general confidence that it will continue through to the next century (Tithe an Oireachtais 1997, 2, 1.3).

Grants available

Forestry grants are available to both the private sector (individual farmers and commercial companies) and to the semi-State forestry company, Coillte Teoranta. Christmas-tree planting, however, is not grant-aided. The rate of financial assistance depends on criteria, determined by the European Union, that include land classification and species to be planted.

- Afforestation Grant
- Forest Premium Grant
- Forest Maintenance Grant
- Forestry Development

Land classification
For the purpose of grant allocation, land is classified into various categories.

Under Council Directives 85/350/EEC and 91/466/EEC, land is categorised by its potential to sustain agricultural produce, as 'more severely handicapped', 'less severely handicapped' and 'non-disadvantaged'. Grants are accordingly tailored to promote different forms of agriculture (including afforestation) in these areas. In addition, land is sub-classified under the Afforestation Grant Scheme (D/AFF 1994b, p. 8, no. 4.2) as follows:

Unenclosed: 'Land which was never improved or enclosed by man-made boundaries for agricultural use other than for extensive grazing' (*ibid.*).

Enclosed/Improved: 'Land falling outside the category of Unenclosed Land' (*ibid.*).

Afforestation Grant Scheme (AGS)
The main grant for planting is the AGS which is available to farmers, landowners and private companies for planting on agricultural land.

The Afforestation Grant Scheme (AGS) is co-financed by the European Union and the Irish Government. The primary objective of the scheme, introduced under European Union Council Regulation 2080/92 as part of the reform of the Common Agricultural Policy (CAP), is to add to the diversity of agricultural land use. It relates to the planting of *agricultural* land and is available in two forms: 1) an afforestation grant for the initial planting, and 2) a maintenance grant, payable four years after the payment of the afforestation grant, for the upkeep of the plantation.

The afforestation grant is the main financial assistance available to landowners and commercial companies alike and provides the bulk of grant-aid for forestry operations. The grant ranges from £975 to £2250 per hectare depending on the type of land and tree species planted. The maintenance grant is available to all applicants except for public authorities, and ranges between £325 and £750 per hectare.

Afforestation Grant Scheme

	Afforestation Grant (£ per ha)	Maintenance Grant (£ per ha)
Unenclosed	975	1300
Enclosed	1125-1350	375-450
Broadleaf/Conifer	1500-1800	500-600
Oak/Beech	1950-2250	650-750

Significant changes have been made to the grant scheme since it was first introduced in 1992, the most relevant of which is the increase in grants available for planting on enclosed and improved land. While there is a minimum area requirement of one hectare (for conifers) and 0.1 hectares (for broadleaves), there is no upper limit to the area which can be planted regardless of land type.

Forest Premium Scheme (FPS)
The FPS is designed specifically to encourage farmers to plant land. It is available only to those who 'suffer a loss of income' because of afforestation of their land (D/AFF 1994b, 4).

Directly associated with the AGS and introduced under the same European Union Directive, the Forest Premium Scheme (FPS) is available for farmers and landowners who 'suffer a loss of income resulting from the afforestation of their land' (*ibid.*, 4). Since it is only available to those in receipt of the AGS, the same conditions and restrictions apply. The premium rate depends on the type of land (enclosed/unenclosed), the type of tree planted (broadleaves/conifers) and the classification of area (non-disadvantaged/handicapped). As with the AGS, the rate of payment for enclosed land is higher than that for unenclosed. The highest payments available are for enclosed land in non-disadvantaged areas.

Forest Premium Scheme

Tree Type	Unenclosed Land (£ per ha)	Enclosed/Improved Land (£ per ha)
Conifers	80-130	100-255
Broadleaves	80-130	120-330

In 1993, 1,378 individual applications were made for grant assistance, of which 95% were between 0-30 hectares in size. Private afforestation of 6,006 hectares of enclosed land and 3,165 hectares of unenclosed land was grant-aided (Irish Timber Growers Association 1995, 102). (Unenclosed land consists largely of upland rough grazing, low marsh, raised and blanket bogs.)

Forestry Development Scheme

Under the Forestry Development scheme, additional grants are available for woodland improvement, publicity/awareness, harvesting machinery, forest roads, research and training (D/AFF 1994a, 132-146). Woodland improvement, for example, covers improvements to degraded or neglected woodland, the development of amenity and urban woodland and the provision of facilities and infrastructure in planned recreational forests (*ibid.*, 132).

CHAPTER 3

Organisations, Policies and Practices

INTRODUCTION
The increasing number of organisations involved in forestry in Ireland make the protection and management of archaeological sites more complex.

Forestry is a relatively new and developing industry in Ireland, supported by the European Union, the Irish Government and private investors. Its impact on agriculture, rural communities, tourism and heritage issues has yet to be fully realised, but it has drawn both positive and negative comment from various sectors. There is frequently confusion about the organisations and policies involved in archaeology and forestry in Ireland which, in turn, can lead to inefficient and frustrating handling of a situation. Increasingly, there is a need for contact and co-operation between the various organisations within the two sectors. The following is an outline of the main policies and policy-makers which govern the two sectors at present.

DEPARTMENT OF ARTS, HERITAGE, THE GAELTACHT AND THE ISLANDS
The Department is responsible for policy formation with respect to heritage issues.

The Department of Arts, Culture and the Gaeltacht was responsible for archaeological policies between 1993 and 1997. That responsibility now rests with the Department of Arts, Heritage, the Gaeltacht and the Islands (D/AHGI), whose Policy Section develops and co-ordinates Government policy on heritage matters. In 1994, the Government introduced an amendment to the National Monuments Acts which established a Record of Monuments and Places. Sites entered into the Record are legally protected from interference without the consent of the Minister. Anyone intending to carry out work that is likely to affect a Recorded Monument must notify the D/AHGI of their intention to do so two months in advance.

In relation to forestry activities, this effectively means that anyone (whether landowners, foresters, farmers or contractors) working in the vicinity of a listed monument must not interfere in any way with the site without notifying the NMHPS of their intention to do so.

Compilation of the Record is the responsibility of the National Monuments and Historic Properties Service, which is also responsible for the implementation of its protective measures.

NATIONAL MONUMENTS AND HISTORIC PROPERTIES SERVICE (NMHPS)
The NMHPS is responsible for the implementation of government policies on archaeology. It is also responsible for issuing archaeological excavation licences, for ensuring that adequate standards of archaeological practice are maintained, and for updating and expanding the archaeological record. In addition, all forestry grant applications that involve archaeological sites are referred to the NMHPS, whose recommendations are taken into consideration by the

In 1996, the heritage services of the Office of Public Works (OPW) were transferred to the Department of Arts, Culture and the Gaeltacht (now the D/AHGI). The NMHPS now acts as the implementing body for the Department's policies, and has statutory responsibility for the protection of archaeology, including sites in forestry. It also liaises with Planning Authorities on developments (such as afforestation) that are likely to affect archaeological sites. Where excavation is considered to be the appropriate course of action, the NMHPS, in conjunction with the National Museum of Ireland (NMI), issues a licence to excavate or undertakes excavation of sites. The NMHPS is also responsible for the operation of the countrywide programme of surveying, updating and distributing Sites and Monuments Records and for the compilation of The Archaeological Survey of Ireland.

The administration of forestry grants requires the Forest Service to check the proposed area for planting against the SMR map for the area. If an

Forest Service.

archaeological site is indicated, the application is passed on to the NMHPS for 'their observation' (Forest Service a). The majority of recommendations are made on the basis of records held in the NMHPS. Between 350 and 400 grant applications from the private sector are screened each year through this process. The usual recommendation is that an area of 15m should be left unplanted around the site but this will obviously vary depending on the type of site. In exceptional cases, where a site is either too extensive or too sensitive, a recommendation to refuse the grant will be made (B. Duffy, pers. comm.). Coillte also forwards maps of areas it proposes to purchase, plant, fell or replant to the NMHPS for comments and recommendations. In 1994, for example, *c.* 250 separate proposals from Coillte for felling and replanting were screened. Due to the current staffing level and the structure of the NMHPS, however, proposed areas for planting are not normally inspected by an official representative in the field.

The NMHPS and the NMI are responsible (on behalf of the D/AHGI) for issuing licences to excavate archaeological and suspected archaeological sites. Apart from monitoring of small-scale excavations that are carried out for non-archaeological purposes, all archaeological monitoring and excavations must be licensed. The applicant must be suitably qualified and experienced in order to obtain a licence; the qualification is judged by a panel representing the D/AHGI through the NMHPS and the NMI. In addition, an application for an excavation licence must be accompanied by a 'method statement' detailing the purpose of the excavation and the approach to be taken on the site. On completion of the excavation, the licensed archaeologist is required to submit a detailed report to the NMHPS and the NMI.

Private and contract archaeologists
There are no specific regulations governing practices or procedures for unlicensed archaeological assessments made by a private or contract archaeologist.

There are an increasing number of archaeologists working in a private capacity throughout Ireland, particularly in pre-development Environmental Impact Assessments. Given the current freelance situation, it is difficult to determine the number of forestry companies that have involved archaeologists in developments. Of 26 private companies and co-operatives questioned in the course of this research, only one reported having employed an archaeologist to carry out pre-afforestation fieldwork. While other examples probably exist, the overall lack of involvement reflects the lack of planning control over afforestation. It remains to be seen how the revised EIA regulations and the introduction of a notification system will affect the situation.

In addition to the lack of input from archaeologists, there are no standards or specific requirements in place for unlicensed archaeological inspection or surveying. It is therefore possible that inexperienced archaeologists are carrying out field assessment and surveying (see Byrnes 1992). Similarly, the standard of the archaeological assessment and reporting of the results has not been adequate. Glenasack Forestry Ltd., for example, employed an archaeologist on several occasions as a consultant, and for carrying out pre-planting field surveys (R. Tobin, pers. comm.); the details of the work, however, were not submitted to the NMHPS and therefore cannot be assessed.

If the impact of forestry developments on archaeological sites is to be controlled in an effective and professional manner, standard procedures and practices will have to be implemented. While the majority of archaeologists will voluntarily maintain high standards, it is essential that the profession as a whole implements guidelines for archaeological monitoring and assessment. Cooney (1991, 79) recommended that a code of practice for contract archaeologists should be formulated. In 1997, the European Association of Archaeologists adopted such a code, and included a significant clause which stipulates that archaeologists should not undertake projects for which they are not adequately trained or prepared (*IAPA Newsletter*, No. 25, 13-14, 1997). While monitoring of large-scale developments and excavations require licences, it is likely that field assessments and EIAs are still being carried out by inexperienced personnel.

Irish Association of Professional Archaeologists (IAPA)
In 1992, IAPA reported that 132 instances of damage to archaeological sites by forestry were identified from a survey of its members.

The Irish Association of Professional Archaeologists (IAPA) has long called for a review of forestry practices with respect to archaeology in Ireland. In 1991 a sub-committee of the Association issued a report on archaeology and forestry (Foley *et al.* 1991). The results of a survey carried out amongst IAPA members revealed that a total of 132 sites were known to be destroyed, damaged or under threat from forestry. Thirty percent of these sites were not marked on Ordnance Survey maps (*ibid.*, 2). This was the first attempt made to quantify the impact of forestry on archaeology and the results act as an important indication of the damage being caused to archaeology by afforestation.

The recommendations made by Foley *et al.* were reinforced by a further document, 'Strategy for the Development of the Forestry Sector in Ireland' (IAPA 1994). The following is a summary of the overall IAPA recommendations:

The role of SMRs

- All available sources of information must be consulted (not just SMRs) and rapid field-based assessment, by a professional archaeologist, must take place for all proposed planting over a suggested 8 hectares. In addition, a pre-afforestation field unit should be established.

EIA threshold

- The threshold for EIAs must be reduced to 100 hectares or lower and adequate standards must be employed.

Management of archaeological sites in forestry

- IAPA (Foley *et al.* 1991, 10, no. 3) called for a policy to facilitate the 'protection of landscape complexes' in addition to introducing management prescriptions for individual sites in forestry. Both reports identify the need to assess and monitor sites in existing forestry (*ibid.*, no. 1(b); IAPA 1994).

Conservation

- IAPA (*ibid.*, no. 5) suggests that a percentage of land owned by forestry companies should be set aside for 'conservation purposes' and that there should be greater contact between nature conservation groups and IAPA.

Professional archaeologist

- The document also recommends that Coillte Teoranta employ a full-time archaeologist to manage sites on its land.

Of the recommendations made by IAPA, only the planting threshold requiring an EIS has been lowered and that occurred mainly in response to pressure from the environment sector and the Department of the Environment.

IAPA has also proposed guidelines for the professional practice of archaeology (IAPA 1995), which stress the need for appropriate standards to be maintained and methodologies to be employed in assessing sites of archaeological potential (*ibid.*, 14-17). Such guidelines need to be developed and adopted by all archaeologists and not just by IAPA members. The document also suggests that a clear distinction must be made between those who have taken archaeology 'to a degree level' and 'the gaining of a qualification as an archaeologist (practitioner)', that is, a professional archaeologist (*ibid.*, 11). The report notes that 'Coillte, for example, have been able to claim they have availed of professional archaeological advice (from staff members with degrees in archaeology)'.

The Heritage Council
The Heritage Council is charged with the practical management and administration of formulating policies on heritage issues. Concern about the potential impact of afforestation on archaeological sites led to this research as a basis for formulating policy and recommendations for future action.

The Heritage Council is a state-sponsored, statutory organisation whose members are appointed from a variety of backgrounds including archaeology. The Council has a statutory responsibility to propose policies and priorities for the identification, protection, preservation and enhancement of the national heritage, and has four main concerns — archaeology, architecture, wildlife and waterways. The Council is a statutory planning consultee. With respect to archaeology, the Heritage Council has assumed the role of the National Monuments Advisory Committee and the statutory responsibilities of the Advisory Committee outlined in the 1930 National Monuments Act. The Council has three primary functions: 1) collecting data on Ireland's Heritage, 2) promoting pride in Ireland's Heritage, and 3) proposing policy and providing advice on Ireland's Heritage.

Arguably, the most significant role of the Heritage Council is its independent status which allows it to operate in a wider capacity than Government Departments. As a statutory body, it has direct input into Government Departments as well as having the power to seek representation on local and National bodies where heritage is an issue. The Council is concerned with developing policies on a wide range of heritage issues that are not adequately catered for under current guidelines and regulations. The impact of the forestry programme on archaeological sites is one such issue.

An Taisce
An Taisce is a non-statutory body which has considerable influence on heritage issues. While An Taisce's concern about forestry is primarily from an environmental perspective, the organisation includes protection of archaeology as an associated issue.

An Taisce is the National Trust for Ireland whose concerns range from architectural heritage to protection of the environment in its broadest sense, including archaeology. An Taisce has a statutory role in Planning Legislation and its recommendations, submitted to various government and local council organisations, can have considerable influence on decisions made. It has also been involved in informal consultation in a few planned forestry schemes (Hickie 1990, 25).

In 1990, An Taisce published a policy document, 'Forestry in Ireland', which dealt with forestry on a comprehensive basis ranging from its economic viability to environmental concerns and conflicts. The document suggested that planting on peatland, particularly along the Atlantic seaboard, was not only environmentally undesirable but that planting of western blanket bogs could be expedient only in achieving short-term, financially motivated targets (*ibid.*, 27). It advocated an amendment to the grant system which would shift the emphasis away from sensitive upland bogs and heather moorland and which would reduce the conflict between forestry and traditional land use. In addition to redressing grant allocations, An Taisce recommended wide-scale implementation of Indicative Forestry Strategies. Both issues have since been addressed and are being implemented.

A further recommendation was that an in-house advisory unit should be established for environmental issues (*ibid.*, 29). This has been addressed, to some extent, by the appointment of Environmental Officers to the major planting company, Coillte, and by research co-ordinated by COFORD.

DEPARTMENT OF THE MARINE AND NATURAL RESOURCES (D/MNR)
The D/MNR is responsible for forestry-related matters.

The Department of Agriculture, Food and Forestry (D/AFF) was responsible for formulating government policy on forestry from 1993 to 1997, during which time significant changes in forestry policy and practice were introduced. Initially forestry appeared to sit uncomfortably within the D/AFF, but it became increasingly accepted as an 'alternative source of income for farmers' (D/AFF 1994a, 14). The relationship between forestry and agriculture is still immature but the number of farmers involved in planting grew significantly between 1993 and 1997.

In 1997, responsibility for forestry was transferred to the Department of the Marine and Natural Resources (D/MNR). It remains to be seen how the shift will affect the recent trends, but the general emphasis on promoting farm-based forestry will probably remain in place. The D/AFF emphasised the significant role of forestry in agricultural and rural development, identifying farm income and rural employment as the main targets for the potential benefits, and presumably that attitude will persist in the new Department.

The D/MNR is also responsible for implementing European Union directives with respect to forestry and is ultimately responsible for ensuring that forestry does not adversely impact on the environment and on archaeology. Government policies on forestry are implemented through the Forest Service which is also responsible for overseeing and administering forestry grants. Forestry policies are outlined in two main documents: 1) The Strategic Plan for the Development of Forestry in Ireland, and 2) The Operational Programme for Agriculture, Rural Development and Forestry.

The Strategic Plan for the Development of the Forestry Sector in Ireland
The Strategic Plan forms the basis for future government policy relating to forestry issues. While its main concerns are economic issues, the Plan acknowledges the significance of archaeological sites in forestry.

In 1993, the government commissioned a review of the forestry industry in Ireland. A consultancy team investigated the current situation and produced a comprehensive programme for the development of the forestry industry that will serve as a basis for government policy up to the year 2015. The Strategic Plan advocates reinforcement of the established planting patterns for the next two decades and retains the ultimate target of a 17% (1.189 million hectares) forest cover by the year 2030 (D/AFF 1996, 3). This target is to be achieved by an annual afforestation rate of approximately 25,000 hectares to the year 2000, and 20,000 hectares thereafter (*ibid.*, 29, 4.1.22). The Plan suggests that approximately 10% of land otherwise suitable for afforestation will be excluded because of environmental restrictions including 'the existence of archaeological sites' (*ibid.*, 28, 4.1.15). The Plan highlights the need for integrated educational programmes for forestry courses, including modules on the environment (*ibid.*, 69, 4.14.19).

While its terms of reference concentrated on the economic and social aspects of the forestry industry, the significance of environmental and archaeological protection is acknowledged (*ibid.*, 28, 4.1.15 and 36, 4.3.17). In the course of preparing the Strategic Plan, the committee received over one hundred submissions from various interested groups and sectors, including the Irish Association of Professional Archaeologists, The

National Heritage Council (now The Heritage Council), and An Taisce. Despite such contributions, there are no new policies or recommendations specifically regarding archaeology. The document suggests that the protection of 'environmentally sensitive areas' relies on:

> *'the timely provision to the Department of Agriculture, Food and Forestry [now to the Department of The Marine and Natural Resources] by the relevant authorities of authoritative, up-to-date and specific information and supporting material such as maps, etc. Sensitive...archaeological sites are examples of areas where such information is still underdeveloped' (ibid., 36, 4.3.20).*

The Operational Programme (1994-1999) for Agriculture, Rural Development and Forestry (OP)
The OP represents European and Irish Government policy on forestry. The primary concern of the OP is the contribution of forestry to rural stability and employment. The ultimate target of the OP is to increase forest cover to 10% by the year 2000.

Operational Programmes are negotiated between the European Union and Member States to identify and assist priority areas for development, such as the forestry industry in Ireland. Under the 1989-1993 Forestry Operational Programme, almost 83,000 hectares (*c.* 200,000 acres) of new planting took place in Ireland with £163 million of European Union and Irish Government grants. The priority status of the Irish forestry sector is reinforced by the current 'Operation Programme 1994-1999 for Agriculture, Rural Development and Forestry' (D/AFF 1994a). This provides for funds of £111 million, with an additional £228 million available under accompanying measures of the CAP Reform. Although financial assistance is available to forestry companies, it is primarily targeted towards promoting forestry as a 'new means of diversifying' farm enterprises and providing additional income for farmers (*ibid.*, 23). Emphasis is also placed on promoting forestry as an industry that contributes to the stability of rural settlements by creating employment. An annual planting target of 30,000 hectares (*c.* 74,130 acres) was established as one of the main objectives outlined by the Programme (*ibid.*, 128), with the ultimate aim of increasing forest cover to over 10% by the year 2000. The annual planting target has since been modified by the Strategic Plan to *c.* 25,000 hectares; otherwise, the policies of the Operational Programme remain largely unchanged.

THE FOREST SERVICE
The Forest Service, under the D/MNR, implements forestry policies and administers grants for forestry in Ireland. The Forest Service has regional Inspectors who oversee grant applications and subsequent planting. The Inspectors are also responsible for protecting archaeology from grant-assisted planting.

The Forest Service is an operational section of the D/MNR and is responsible for implementing European and Government forestry policies in Ireland. It oversees operation of the forestry programme and administers all applications for grant-aided tree planting. The Forest Service is responsible for the protection of Irish forests and is, ultimately, responsible for development and research in the field. Training and information courses for farmers on forest establishment are also organised by the Forest Service in conjunction with Teagasc.

The Forest Service operates from a central Dublin office with 16 Regional Inspectors to oversee afforestation programmes in the 26 counties. The Inspectors are responsible for processing grant applications and regulating grant-aided planting. Between 1992 and 1995, approximately 5,300 individual applications were processed, and with over 20,000 hectares of planting per annum, the resources of the Forest Service are stretched to the limit. As a result, practical concerns cannot always be addressed at ground level. The government decision to allow self-regulation for six of the main forestry companies (with occasional Forest Service spot-checks) undoubtedly relieved the pressure somewhat but the increase in private and farm planting has more than burdened them again. In an attempt to relieve some of the work-load, Teagasc will play an increasingly important role in advising farmers with respect to forestry (D/AFF 1996, 41).

While the policies outlined in the Strategic Plan and the Operational Pro-gramme acknowledge the potentially adverse effects of forestry on archae-ological sites, specific policy with respect to archaeology in forestry is more clearly defined with reference to the Forest Service. The 'Forestry and Archaeology Guidelines' leaflet (Forest Service, a), which is issued to each grant-applicant, summarises the legal position with respect to archaeolog-ical monuments and forestry, and outlines procedures for protecting sites during planting and felling operations. These guidelines must be adhered to in order to quality for all forestry grants. (An updated version of 'For-estry and Archaeology Guidelines' is being compiled and is due to be pub-lished in mid-1998. It is assumed that the revised version will amend the information on the National Monuments Acts, the Record of Monuments and Places, and the recent changes in planning laws.) The current guide-lines provide brief descriptions and illustrations of some of the most com-mon archaeological monument types. While acknowledging the limitations of space in a leaflet, it is noteworthy that the guidelines do not mention early prehistoric, sub-soil sites or later historical sites such as mills, lime kilns and vernacular architecture. Whether or not the revised guidelines will include such sites remains to be seen.

The following summarises the Forest Service's procedures and practices which apply to all grant-aided afforestation:

Recorded (SMR) sites

- Forest Service Inspectors check the proposed planting area against the SMR maps and refer any potentially affected site to the NMHPS.

Sensitive areas

- Grant approvals preclude the planting of 'sensitive sites'.

Training of staff

- Inspectors 'will be trained with the help of the NMHPS to assist them in identifying areas of possible archaeological importance not previously recorded'.

Buffer zones

- An 'appropriate' buffer zone must be left unplanted around an archaeological site and the site must be protected from all forest activity.

Access to sites

- An additional unplanted zone must be left along any existing access route.

Demarcation of sites

- The area around a site should be marked out with stakes, clearly identifying the site as a protected area.

Excavation

- Where a 'rescue excavation' is required it will be carried out at the developer's expense.

Reporting of artefacts

- Artefacts found during work must be reported to the Gardaí or the Director of the National Museum.

Harvesting and thinning

- Sites in existing woodland must be protected during felling and thin-ning operations and machine operators must be advised of the pres-ence of an archaeological site.

Field assessment
Forest Service Inspectors carry out spot-checks to assess implementation of the guidelines.

Regardless of how well-structured the revised guidelines might be, their implementation is fraught with practical difficulties. The Forest Service Inspectors carry out spot-checks to ensure compliance with the guidelines. The degree of non-compliance is not known, but given the current over-strained resources of the Forest Service, it is likely that a significant proportion of archaeological sites are rarely inspected more than once (if at all) during the life cycle of the forest. Site inspection occurs on a sampling basis of one in three, prior to grant approval, and one in three before grant payment (Tithe an Oireachtais 1997, 45, 11.8). To assess the overall degree of compliance with the Forest Service guidelines on archaeology, a detailed field-based assessment is required either as a specific survey or as part of a more broad-based assessment.

Assessment of sites at local level
In the absence of local-level archaeological consultation and assessment, the current system of assessment operates through central offices in Dublin. This is both time-consuming and of limited practical use, given the lack of opportunity it affords for archaeological inspection of sites in the field.

According to the Forest Service, grant-applications that do not have environmental or archaeological implications are usually processed at local level within two months. When a proposed area includes a recorded archaeological site, however, some farming organisations have claimed that planting approval can take up to seven months (*Irish Farmers Journal*, April 8th, 1995). There is considerable pressure on the Forest Service to speed up the process and one suggestion is that all applications should be approved at a local level. While the number of archaeologists working with local authorities is increasing, Ireland does not have a formal system of local or regional archaeologists with authority to inspect sites and advise on archaeological issues. Without the presence of a regional archaeologist, or the equivalent, there is no official alternative but to refer the application to the NMHPS offices in Dublin. It has been suggested that the NMHPS should supply the Forest Service with maps of archaeological sites, colour-coded on the basis of sensitivity, importance, etc., effectively excluding official archaeological approval (*ibid.*). The introduction of a notification system whereby the Forest Service informs the relevant local authority of applications to plant over 25 hectares of land may result in an improvement of the situation. Given the increasingly significant role of archaeologists within local authorities, it may ultimately be possible to provide advice and information on the archaeological aspects of the grant application at a local level. At present, however, the procedures for assessing the implications of grant-aided forestry applications remain cumbersome and limited in their effectiveness.

Identifying and protecting archaeological sites in grant-aided forestry
In the majority of cases, an adequate buffer zone around a monument will suffice to ensure its protection. Some sites will, however, require attention throughout the forest cycle. Continued protection of the site must be a condition of grant-assistance. Unrecorded archaeological sites are most at risk from afforestation and the guidelines must stress the fact that many sites have yet to be discovered.

The presence of an archaeological site will not usually preclude an applicant from planting. In the majority of cases a buffer zone maintained free of overgrowth around the monument will suffice to protect it. Where an archaeological site is extensive, it is essential that it is inspected by a suitably experienced archaeologist so that an informed decision can be made regarding the possibility of planting. The full extent of a site might not be obvious at ground level, or to an inexperienced individual. At present, the staffing levels and the structure of the archaeological authorities permit such assessment only in exceptional cases. Although the Forest Service advocates training for its Inspectors on how to recognise sites in the field (Forest Service, a), Cooney (1993, 15) notes that the Forest Service guidelines may give the impression that SMRs are complete records of the archaeology of an area. Sites that are not recorded are most at risk from afforestation. The recently introduced notification system for local authorities should improve the rate of detection of previously unrecorded archaeology in some areas; it relies, however, on continuous interaction and consultation between the local authority, professional archaeologists, and the Forest Service. Given the difficulty of predicting where archaeological sites are likely to occur, a system for monitoring planting preparation needs to be introduced and the Forest Service guidelines must allow for this possibility. Landowners also need to be encouraged to identify unrecorded sites as well as to actively manage known sites within their plantations. The current financial incentive to plant (planting and maintenance grants, tax-free profits for the harvest, etc.) should provide adequate compensation for facilitating protection of archaeological sites. The protective measures, however, must be enforced in practice.

While recorded archaeological sites are legally protected from unauthorised interference, this is unlikely to give adequate protection in practice. Whether through accident, ignorance or blatant defiance of the law, sites are more likely to be damaged where they are not clearly marked and maintained within a forest. For commercial and private forestry investors, there should be appropriate incentives not to damage archaeological features. If the unplanted area in and around a site was to be formally included in the grant payment, on condition that the buffer zone and access to the site be maintained, it would raise awareness of archaeological sites and ensure greater protection of the site during the forest cycle.

Demarcation of archaeological sites
While Forest Service guidelines require clear marking of the boundary of archaeological sites, fieldwork suggests that this is rarely carried out. A standardised form of staking, and cordoning-off where necessary, is required.

Given the increasing use of contractors at various stages in the forest cycle, it is essential that archaeological sites should be clearly marked in the field before and during all forestry activities, as outlined by the Forest Service guidelines. This guideline is particularly significant during planting preparation, felling and harvesting activities when large machinery is involved and sites may be obscured by vegetation. The elementary fieldwork carried out in the course of this research and previously documented examples of damage to sites, however, suggest that clear marking of the boundaries of sites rarely occurs. Where stakes are used in the initial stages of planting operations, they are frequently overgrown and rendered invisible by subsequent vegetation growth. The fieldwork was not extensive or specific enough to determine the overall level of adherence to the guidelines, but it highlighted this aspect as one which requires further investigation.

It is accepted that grant-driven agricultural practices are temporary and unsustainable and that once excessive production is reduced in one area, the emphasis will again change. Grants often exist in conflict with each other so that, for example, while the Department of Agriculture has offered grants to drain, fertilise and reclaim land, the Department of the Environment has simultaneously offered incentives to avoid such activities. While there are many potentially negative aspects of agricultural grants, there is one important benefit for archaeology, that is, they allow some control over the impact of land-use changes on sites and monuments. The significance for archaeology of having additional guidelines governing grant-aided activities is the potential to monitor and control such operations as planting. Throughout the 1970s and 80s, land reclamation, for example, was heavily assisted by EEC/government grants. Cooney (1991, 75) notes that 'because the trend now is for land reclamation largely to be carried out without the benefit of grant-aid, monitoring of the archaeological impact is more difficult'. At present, grants for afforestation can be withheld or refused where Forest Service guidelines are not adhered to. In theory, if a recorded monument or site in grant-assisted forestry is damaged, the landowner can be fined up to £50,000 and/or imprisoned, in addition to having the grant reclaimed by the Forest Service. In practice, given the overall lack of archaeological inspection, it is unlikely that many cases of non-compliance will be detected.

Non-grant-assisted planting
Private planting which is not grant-assisted is outside the brief of the Forest Service. While it comprises a small percentage of the overall afforestation, a system of monitoring archaeological sites within such forests needs to be developed.

While the provisions of the National Monuments Acts apply to all cases of planting, the specific requirement to allow an unplanted buffer zone around an existing site applies only to planting which is grant-assisted. Relative to grant-aided planting, the percentage of non-grant-aided planting is minuscule, but there is one significant market which deserves some attention. Growing of Christmas trees is not, and will not be, grant-assisted, but the increasing export market attracts more companies into the sector annually. Christmas trees generally require better-quality soils than other commercial species and therefore much of their distribution is on land where archaeological settlement sites might be expected. The methods of planting Christmas trees (as with all trees) depend on the ground conditions as well as the species. The most common planting techniques used are pit-planting, ploughing and mounding (where the soil is wet). Where the technique is invasive, or where drainage systems are to be constructed, monitoring and field assessment of such operations will have to be introduced.

Given the lack of Forest Service control over non-grant-assisted afforestation, the establishment of a system for monitoring and assessing archaeology in such cases will probably be more complex. It is possible, however, to identify companies involved in planting Christmas trees and therefore spot-checks could be carried out by authorised archaeologists, particularly in areas which have, or are thought likely to have, archaeological sites. While an unplanted buffer zone is not a legal requirement, it is the only practical method of avoiding damage to a site in forestry. Therefore, in most cases, those who plant trees too close to a recorded site will be in breach of the law by causing damage to, or destroying, the site.

Recreational Forestry Scheme
There is considerable potential for managing and promoting archaeological sites in forestry with the assistance of schemes such as the Recreational Forestry Scheme.

The Strategic Plan for the Development of the Forestry Sector in Ireland acknowledges the potential benefits of multi-functional or recreational forestry and identifies it as an increasingly important aspect of Irish forestry. The Plan notes that 'an attractive forest feature...can attract additional visitors into an area and thus provide a boost to the local economy' (D/AFF 1996, 46, 4.6.8).

Gardiner (1991, 351) recommends that provisions for enhancing the forest environment or promoting environmental features within forestry should be made 'in any incentive scheme'. Provision is made for amenity, educational and environmental issues through the 1992 Planned Recreational Forestry Scheme (D/AFF 1994a, 133). The Forest Service operates the grant-aided scheme which offers financial assistance for forestry grown or maintained for the purposes of public education and leisure activities. The Operational Programme targeted 1,000 hectares as 'Planned Recreation' woodlands and provides a maximum of £1,000 per hectare for developing such land (*ibid.*, 134). A further measure exists for promoting forestry 'as a key area of economic and social advantage and which contributes favourably to the environment' (*ibid.*, 136). Recreational forests must include up to one third of the total area free of tree cover in order to qualify for the grant. Through co-ordinated and co-operative means, existing archaeological sites could be incorporated into such woodlands with appropriate protective measures in place where necessary. A similar scheme, the Amenity

Woodland Scheme, launched in 1996, also encourages landowners to include recreational and leisure activities in woodlands, placing emphasis on the improvement and use of old woodlands (D/AFF 1996, 45, 4.6.5).

COILLTE TEORANTA
Coillte Teoranta owns and manages all State forestry, making it the largest land and forest owner in Ireland. With so much land under its control, the company plays an important role in the management of archaeology.

Under the 1988 Forestry (Amendment) Act, ownership and practical management of all State forests was transferred from the Department of Energy to a newly established, semi-State forestry company, Coillte Teoranta. In all, State forests amount to about 400,000 hectares (1,056,825 acres) of land, making Coillte the largest land owner in the country with an estimated asset value of about £800 million (Gallagher 1995, 13).

Coillte is also the largest single purchaser of land in the country. In 1994, for example, the company acquired 5,998 hectares (14,821 acres) of land for planting and had a target of increasing acquisition by 21% in 1995 to 7,250 hectares (17,915 acres). The figures available for 1995, however, fell short of that target mainly due to the impact of other CAP reform measures and increased competition from other companies and sectors. About 20% of this land was acquired through the Farm Forestry Partnership Scheme which is becoming increasingly popular. Under this scheme, the farmer retains ownership of the land and gets a percentage of the final crop value, while Coillte carries out the establishment and management of the plantation.

Early State planting was concentrated in upland and very marginal soils, but there has been a shift in trends particularly towards wet mineral lowland soils. Coillte has a policy of not acquiring any further intact blanket bog and now concentrates on planting rough pasture land, some of which was reclaimed during the 1970s (J. McLoughlin, pers. comm.). While better-quality soils are generally too expensive to acquire, Coillte carries out some Christmas tree planting on them.

Twelve forest parks and other forest trails and picnic sites are managed by Coillte as public recreation areas (Coillte Teoranta 1992b), with approximately one million pounds spent on providing facilities (Tithe an Oireachtais 1997, 4, 1.6). The company uses the grant scheme for 'Planned Recreational Forests' to provide and improve public awareness of archaeology within these forests. In addition to the development and management of forests, Coillte also has a range of related activities including nurseries, timber processing and forestry research.

Archaeological policy
In response to increasing concerns about the protection of the environment and archaeology, Coillte formulated a company policy which outlines management recommendations and objectives. Coillte, however, does not employ an in-house professional archaeologist, and relies on the Heritage Services of the NMHPS for advice on archaeological matters.

Coillte is by far the largest self-regulating forestry company and, therefore, has a greater responsibility for archaeological sites on its property. The company acknowledges the potential impact of afforestation and forestry activity on archaeology in its environmental policy statement (Coillte Teoranta 1993). It recognises that 'many remaining [archaeological] sites can be on marginal agricultural land, previously unaffected by development, where forestry is the preferred land use' and that the 'wide usage of heavy machinery for ground preparation, road making and extraction can also affect archaeological sites'. Coillte is forthright in acknowledging that 'it would be unacceptable for the Company to allow any sites whether recorded or not to be damaged'. There is, however, a bias in the environmental policy statement, and in general, towards upstanding monuments at the expense of less obvious sites — the only sites mentioned in the statement are those of earth and stone.

To achieve the above objectives, Coillte incorporated details of all known archaeological sites into its Geographical Information System (GIS) as a means of 'ensuring' that sites would be protected from forestry activity (*ibid.*). The company has also appointed Environmental Officers to oversee activities in seven of its regional areas. Part of their brief is the protection of archaeological sites and reporting of sites discovered during planting. Both introductions contribute to the protection of known sites, but neither is adequate for identifying and protecting unrecorded features.

Despite the fact that Coillte is the largest single land-owner in the country, the company does not employ a professional archaeologist on a full-time basis. The company consults with the NMHPS for advice on areas to be planted and land which it proposes to acquire where there is a likelihood of a significant archaeological presence. Coillte policy aims to increase awareness of archaeology within the company and to achieve this it has held seminars and lectures for its field personnel. This is, however, a system that relies on interested individuals rather than on professionals specifically trained to carry out such work.

Contract work
While Coillte has strict regulations in place, it employs a significant number of contractors, rendering monitoring of the regulations and protection of archaeology more difficult.

The current success of the forestry industry is reflected in Coillte's increase in profits which rose from around two million pounds in 1993 to about eleven million in 1994. The dramatic increase is partially the result of a rationalisation programme which has already reduced the workforce from 2,600 seven years ago to about 1,450 in 1994 (Coillte Teoranta 1994). As the company's full-time workforce is reduced, it contracts more work out to private forestry companies and individuals. As more contractors become involved in the planting and harvesting processes, it will obviously become more difficult to monitor and control standards, practices and adherence to Forest Service guidelines.

FORESTRY RESEARCH AND TRAINING
Forestry research and training concentrates on silvicultural issues. While Coillte has held lectures and seminars on archaeology, overall awareness of the subject would be improved by its inclusion in all training schemes and courses.

Primary forestry research is carried out by COFORD (the Council for Forest Research and Development) and financed under a sub-measure of the Operational Programme (D/AFF 1994a, 142-3). Research deals with afforestation issues including environmental aspects and down-stream industrial development. 'Environmental compatibility for all elements of the industry is an essential part' of a substantial research and development programme (Pathway to Progress) co-ordinated by COFORD (Mulloy 1995, 33). The Forest Institute of Remote Sensing Technology (FIRST), in association with the Department of Forestry, University College Dublin, is currently compiling satellite and aerial photographic data for mapping Irish forests and land use. This research should potentially allow complimentary SMR data to be incorporated, giving definitive information on previously recorded archaeological sites in forestry. An integrated system of known archaeological and forestry distribution would provide indicators for sites which require immediate attention, e.g. sites in forests due to be thinned or harvested. These sites could then be identified at ground level and marked clearly to prevent damage during such operations.

To comply with CAP reforms, all agricultural training courses have now been restructured to include modules on environmental protection (D/AFF 1994a, 176). The Strategic Plan for the Development of Forestry in Ireland also identified a need for 'integrated educational and training modules on forestry and the environment (D/AFF 1996, 69, 4.14.19).

Concern has been expressed about the low standards of practice and the lack of training in forest management sometimes encountered in the forestry industry (*ibid.*, 6-7, 1.12). The Irish Timber Growers Association (ITGA), which represents private sector tree farmers, has stressed that the preoccupation with meeting planting targets must take cognisance of the need for high quality training and experienced personnel (*Irish Farmers Journal*, June 17th, 1995). The umbrella group representing a large section of the forestry industry, the Irish Forest Industry Chain (IFIC), has similarly voiced its concern (*Irish Farmers Journal*, April 29th, 1995).

Given that Ireland doesn't have a tradition of forest management, it will be some time before forestry is established as a normal agricultural practice. While the majority of farmers either employ a contractor or one of the main forestry companies to carry out the planting, there is increasing involvement by private individuals who are relatively untrained and inexperienced in managing forests. The significant consequence for archaeology is the danger that neglected or poorly managed forests will completely engulf archaeological sites, preventing access to them and ultimately damaging or destroying them. Lack of training and poor woodland management skills are likely to be matched by an equally uninformed attitude towards any archaeology encountered. There is no statutory requirement for forestry companies to educate their staff in archaeology, nor to employ suitably trained archaeologists. Coillte Teoranta is seemingly exceptional in holding occasional seminars and lectures on archaeology and consulting archaeologists on matters other than those required by the planting regulations.

Teagasc

Teagasc is responsible for research and development in agriculture and has become increasingly involved with the forestry sector.

Teagasc is the government organisation responsible for research, advice and development in agriculture. With the integration of forestry into the agricultural sector, Teagasc is now involved in training, development and practical activities related to forestry. Many of its activities either complement or, increasingly, substitute the role of the Forest Service. Where the demand for advice and assistance in farm forestry is greatest, Teagasc provides the service which would normally be executed by the Forest Service, giving advice on the various aspects of planting. This advisory role is expected to become increasingly significant due to the pressure on the Forest Service resources. Teagasc has Regional Officers, some of whom are acutely aware of archaeological issues and actively involved in protecting archaeology in their area. These officers are particularly important as the first point of contact for farmers involved in farm forestry and in the REP scheme. In addition, Teagasc is recruiting professional forestry staff to advise its field officers, and will further develop forestry training courses with the Forest Service (D/AFF 1996, 42, 4.4.23).

Indicative Forestry Strategy (IFS)

Teagasc has developed a pilot Indicative Forestry Strategy (IFS) which incorporates information from SMRs into a GIS database designed to identify land suitable for forestry. IFSs are considered primarily as planning tools to inform the Forest Service, local authorities and developers of the potential for afforestation in a region. While archaeological sites are a

The Forest Service commissioned Teagasc's Forestry Research Department to develop an Indicative Forestry Strategy in Co. Clare (Bulfin *et al.* 1993, 98). As the name suggests, an Indicative Forestry Strategy (IFS) is a system which identifies and defines characteristics that render land suitable (or unsuitable) for forestry. The pilot IFS incorporated features such as geology, yield potential of the soil, wind-throw hazard levels, archaeology, environmental issues and farming potential. These and other related aspects were included in a Geographical Information System (GIS). The GIS allows information to be manipulated and analysed to determine the suitability of an area before planting permission is granted. It forms a structured plan for forestry, which could be used to indicate to the forestry industry, archaeologists, environmental groups, and other interested parties, where future planting is likely to occur. This would provide local authorities with greater control over development in their areas, and National Authorities with information on which to base their policies with respect to forestry.

IFSs have operated in Scotland for a number of years and were developed to facilitate local planning authorities and private companies in identifying areas where planting permission is likely to be refused (Goodstadt 1991). Scottish IFSs are drawn up in close consultation with the archaeological authorities.

The Irish IFS differs from the Scottish strategy in its overall approach — while Scottish IFSs *exclude* certain areas (soil types, areas of high archaeological potential, etc.) from afforestation plans, the Irish scheme identified potential areas to be *included* in future afforestation (M. Bulfin, pers. comm.). Initially, the Irish scheme included all areas in order to assess their suitability for forestry. Areas such as SMR sites, proposed Natural Heritage Areas, etc. were then isolated. The IFS included all known archaeological sites and monuments from the SMR, allocating a buffer zone of *c.* 20 metres around each site. At present, the IFS is used for checking private applications for planting, i.e. expected yield class, the presence of recorded archaeological sites, etc. It is expected that IFSs will be compiled over the next three years for all counties, providing a data base for the Forest Service of potential areas for planting.

While the IFSs are intended for use by the Forest Service, they are potentially useful tools for archaeologists. The areas identified as being suitable for afforestation could be further assessed for their archaeological potential. In some cases, this might result in prescribing management schemes for individual sites; in others, it might require full-scale investigation of the area. The IFS only incorporates information based on the SMRs. A more detailed assessment would identify some of the areas most likely to be of archaeological potential, for example, areas with a high concentration of particular site-types, marginal and upland areas, or low-lying wet mineral soils where unrecorded sites are likely to exist. While this would involve considerable financial input, it is becoming increasingly obvious that such surveys are required in order to identify and record archaeological sites and landscapes (e.g. the 'Afforestable Land Survey' see p. 78). The lack of research into archaeology in forestry and afforestable settings should not be defended on financial grounds alone.

PRIVATE FORESTRY

While Coillte Teoranta has implemented additional policies regarding archaeology in forestry, the situation with respect to private companies is more difficult to assess and monitor. The most recent inventory of private woodlands in Ireland was compiled in 1973 and identified a total of 81,963 hectares of privately owned forests, of which 42% was considered to be 'scrub woodland' (Neeson 1991, 366). The rate of private planting, however, has risen dramatically since then (Fig. 13). Between 1982 and 1994, for example, over 72,000 hectares of land were planted by the private sector. The Forest Service is currently compiling a new inventory of forestry throughout the country to allow for easier assessment and planning for the forestry industry. At present, while Coillte has a GIS incorporating information on State forestry, there is no up-to-date inventory of private forestry.

There are currently over twenty forestry companies directly involved in tree-planting in the Republic of Ireland. The majority receive grants administered by the Forest Service for establishment, maintenance and related forestry activity (road building, purchase of machinery, etc.) and must therefore adhere to its guidelines on archaeology and forestry. As outlined above, proposed planting which involves an SMR site is referred by the Forest Service to the National Monuments and Historic Properties Service (NMHPS) and appropriate recommendations are made regarding protection for the site. There is, however, no field monitoring or follow-up spot-checks by NMHPS officers to ensure that these recommendations are implemented.

The number of individual cases of private planting is a significant factor in responding to the threat posed to archaeology. Between 1982 and 1994, there were 8,260 cases of grant-aided private planting (Irish Timber Growers Association 1995, 94). They ranged from as few as 17 cases in Co. Louth to 856 cases in Co. Kerry.

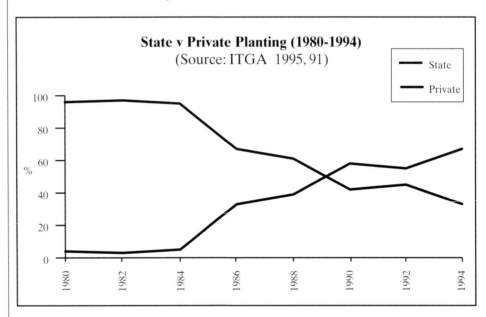

State v Private Planting (1980-1994)
(Source: ITGA 1995, 91)

Fig. 13. *Private and State Afforestation. Private planting rates have risen significantly since the mid-1980s and overtook the rate of State planting in 1989. The introduction of, and increases in, planting grants are reflected by planting rates for 1985/86, 1988/89 and 1993/94.*

Forty per cent of all private planting between 1982 and 1994 took place in Munster, compared with 17% in Leinster, 33.5% in Connaught and 9.2% in Ulster (Republic of Ireland). In 1994, there were 956 cases of farm-based planting and 877 cases of part-time farmers and non-farmers, giving a total of 1,833 individual instances of planting in the Republic. Munster experienced the highest uptake of planting grants with 41% of the number of private cases, against 23.8% in Connaught, 27.4% in Leinster and 7.9% in Ulster, (Republic of Ireland). Given that over 70% of private planting in the past decade has taken place in Munster and Connaught, it is reasonable to suggest that these provinces must be targeted for immediate action.

The increase in private and farm forestry over the past five years has complicated the practical side of site identification and protection. Private management of forestry is an issue which has received considerable attention, and concerns have been expressed that forestry grants for farmers may be viewed by some as 'a substitute for social welfare' resulting in overgrown, impenetrable and generally neglected plantations (*Irish Farmers Journal*, Oct. 21st, 1995). Any archaeology existing in such plantations would undoubtedly suffer as a consequence. While the situation is currently being addressed by government, farm and forestry organisations, it also needs to be monitored from an archaeological perspective.

The distribution of private planting suggests that if the archaeological authorities are to respond, it will have to be at a regional or local level. Assessment from a centralised base is neither practical nor effective. In 1993, for example, there was a total of 1,294 individual cases of planting, of which the NMHPS carried out a paper-based assessment of about 360 (*c.* 28%) (B. Duffy, pers. comm.). While details of these assessments were not available, the general response from the NMHPS is a reiteration of the Forest Service guidelines on providing buffer zones and avoiding damage to the sites.

A study of Environmental Impact Assessments (EIAs) in 1992 reported that of seven EIAs carried out between 1991 and 1992, only one was commissioned by a private developer (Byrnes 1992, 19). That EIA was considered to be 'the poorest example', providing no details of the archaeological survey, which apparently relied solely on the SMR information. It would appear that with the introduction of new planning regulations and notification requirements the situation is improving. In addition, the lowering of the threshold from 200 to 70 hectares should result in an increased number of EIAs.

Farm forestry
The attitudes of farmers towards forestry varies from active involvement to utter disdain. Farm-based planting is now, however, an important sector of the forestry industry.

The proportion of private afforestation has risen dramatically from 4% in 1980 to 73% in 1995, with farm-based forestry accounting for 62% (D/AFF 1996, 39, 4.4.1). Despite the increasing numbers of farmers involved in forestry, there is still a considerable amount of uncertainty and scepticism amongst rural communities. In many areas a traditional disdain for trees and particularly for coniferous plantations is evident. The isolation of farms and farm houses surrounded by closely planted trees is of concern to most rural residents. While the major farming organisations recognise the potential benefits of farm-based forestry, they have called for tighter controls and greater planning in establishing plantations. The United Farmers Association (UFA), for example, advocates the imposition of an EIA for all planting over one hectare. The Irish Creamery Milk Suppliers Association (ICMSA) has called for 'specific rules and regulations' controlling planting over 20 acres (Allen 1996). Their common concerns include the increasing competition between farmers and forestry companies for land, the isolating effect of blanket afforestation on farms, the impact of forestry on the environment, landscape and tourism, and the overall absence of a national land-use policy.

Irish Farmers' Association (IFA)
The IFA is the largest and most influential farming organisation in Ireland. Its policies, therefore, will have a significant impact on archaeology. The IFA-proposed land-use policy

The Irish Farmers' Association (IFA) is the largest and probably the most influential representative group for Irish farming. Concern about the rate of afforestation and the need for a 'review and reform' of land-use policy led to the establishment within the IFA of a Forestry Review Committee which contributed to the land-use policy document submitted to Government in January 1995 (Irish Farmers' Association 1995). In line with other

argued for a restructuring of forestry policy to encourage farm-based planting. It also suggested that penalties for breaches of the forestry guidelines were not being imposed.

interested parties, the IFA acknowledges the potential benefits of forestry as an additional source of income for its members.

In January 1995, the IFA submitted a land-use policy document to government (*ibid.*). One of the main concerns of that document was the impact of current forestry policy on land use. In addition, they considered the effect of increasing afforestation on the 'physical and social environment'. Those recommendations which potentially involve archaeological issues are summarised as follows:

- To balance the forestry premium scheme in favour of farmers;

- To maintain the 200 ha threshold for requirement of an EIA;

- To restructure the processes involved in carrying out EIAs;

- To reinforce the 'conditions of eligibility' for grant payments, i.e. where guidelines are not adhered to, grant payment ought to be withheld;

- That notification of a change in land use from agriculture to forestry should be made publicly with an appeals mechanism in place for local objections to be considered.

The most recent trend towards planting of good-quality farm land is also of concern to the IFA. While the organisation is not in favour of planning control (because of the bureaucratic nature of planning), they have suggested 'some form of land use agency...along the lines of the old Land Commission' (*Irish Farmers Journal*, March 30th, 1996).

The IFA, in general, promotes awareness and protection of the natural and cultural environment and encourages its members to balance those concerns with the practicalities of farming. Ultimately, however, its priorities are necessarily economic viability for its members, which will sometimes adversely affect archaeology. The IFA initially objected to the reduction in the EIA threshold, fearing that additional costs would be incurred for farmers establishing plantations. It has now welcomed the reduction but wants exemptions for farmers planting next to established forestry. Environmental Impact Assessments are undoubtedly a costly element of forest establishment with an average cost of about £100 per hectare (*Irish Farmers Journal*, April 6th, 1996). While the larger forest companies can obviously carry these costs, it is understandable that some farmers are concerned about the revised regulations. Given the small size of the average area planted by private sector, however, it is unlikely to be an issue for the majority of farmers.

Forestry co-operatives
The development of forestry co-ops is a potentially useful point of contact for archaeologists and farmers. Where planting occurs in a wide-spread area but in small land parcels, co-operatives could prove useful for promoting archaeological awareness and for co-ordinating archaeological impact assessments where necessary.

As forestry becomes more profitable and more forestry co-operatives are established, land is gradually being consolidated as large land packages, particularly in marginal zones. Co-operatives such as Western Forestry Co-operative, based in Sligo, are being developed along the lines of the established Danish forestry co-operatives, which provide advice, support and practical assistance to farmers who want to get involved in forestry. The Western Forestry Co-op, a European Union funded organisation, has succeeded in planting around 5,000 hectares (*c.* 12,400 acres) in the first five years of operation. One of the primary aims of the co-op is to prevent planting of the relatively scarce good-quality land in the West of Ireland by targeting the poorer-quality lands in marginal areas (*Irish Farmers Journal*, May 20th, 1995). Much of the planting in this area is done by FÁS-trained workers. The development of forestry co-operatives means that small, fragmented holdings in the West can be consolidated into larger tracts of land, encouraging more farmers to plant marginal agricultural land. The organisation of forestry co-operatives is encouraging farmers to group together and share the costs of planting and harvesting these fragmented areas. Avonmore Farm Forestry Service, part of the Avonmore Co-operative, has an arrangement with Coillte to strengthen planting, management, commercial strategies, etc. It also establishes regional co-operatives to promote farm-based forestry, for example, Donaghmore Farm Forestry Co-operative.

Given the practical difficulties of protecting archaeological sites, the introduction of forestry co-operatives may be a potentially useful development. If direct contact between the co-operatives and archaeologists is established, such organisations may prove useful in ensuring that archaeology is given due consideration when farmers are planning their forestry. Some co-operatives are already active in promoting and preserving heritage. The Monasteraden Resources Co-operative in Co. Sligo, for example, views forestry as one aspect of an integrated development programme for their region (*ibid.*). The programme has included archaeological excavation of two crannógs on the lake shore of Lough Gara.

ENVIRONMENTAL ISSUES

Archaeology is seen as falling within broader environmental issues. While the two areas have many common concerns, they are, ultimately, separate issues and must be dealt with accordingly. Contact and co-ordinated management schemes, however, would be of benefit to both areas.

The relationship between archaeology and environmental issues such as nature conservation has been described as 'complicated, but close' (Macinnes 1993, 248). While emphasising the association between environmental and archaeological considerations, it is also necessary to deal with the conflicts of interests which may arise. A broadleaf forest, for example, can cause as much damage to archaeology as its evergreen counterpart and the same archaeological conditions need to be applied in both cases: pre-planting assessment, monitoring of planting, etc. Similarly, overgrowth by vegetation in the unplanted buffer zones around archaeological sites in forestry may add diversity to the forest environment, but is undesirable from an archaeological perspective. However, concern about development in rural areas and the ultimate objective of protecting certain aspects of the landscape is shared.

While archaeological and environmental interests share a common concern about afforestation, their methods of dealing with the subject have differed considerably. Until recently, the greatest objections to afforestation have come from environmental and ecological groups who argue that commercial evergreen plantations destroy or reduce diversity in wildlife, damage the natural soil structure and water levels, and contribute nothing to the environment. Such objections are frequently voiced through the media and both public and political awareness of the conflict is relatively high.

The forestry sector is fully aware of the potentially negative impact of forestry on the environment (e.g. Farrell 1993). It is also aware of public pressure and has tried to fit forestry into its surroundings in a sensitive and appropriate manner (e.g. McLoughlin 1996; O'Halloran and Giller 1993; McCormack and O'Leary 1993; Forest Service b).

Archaeology has taken a quieter route in arguing for tighter controls, but it has also benefited from some of the environmental protection legislation. Environmental Impact Assessments, for example, include archaeological evaluation as part of the process and are now required for planting over 70 hectares of land. Similarly, the recent introduction of a notification system for planting over 25 hectares should prove beneficial to archaeology. The introduction of Environmental Officers in Coillte has also raised the awareness of archaeology within the company. While other environmental designations do not specifically require archaeological protection, they have the potential to benefit archaeology indirectly by limiting afforestation in sensitive landscapes.

Environmental designations
Ireland is obliged to protect sites of European importance as Special Protection Areas (SPAs) or Special Areas of Conservation (SACs). These areas will be afforded special protection from developments which would have negative environmental consequences, including afforestation. While archaeology within such areas will be protected from development, legal protection is limited and a lack of management plans may affect protection.

Nature conservation is protected by the European Union through directives such as 79/409/EEC and 92/43/EEC on the protection of birds and natural habitats. Any land considered to be internationally valuable under the terms of these directives must be protected and grants for afforestation are not available. In Ireland, approximately 5% of the land area falls under this category. In addition, European forestry grants are not generally available for planting on 'important peatlands' as defined by the Irish Peatland Conservancy Council and an estimated 200,000 hectares of blanket bog in the Republic are thereby protected.

The most recent environmental designation, proposed Natural Heritage Areas (NHAs), brings the amount of protected land to about 8%. A diversity of habitats is involved in the proposed NHAs, some of which have no archaeological significance (e.g. a tiny bat habitat), but others of which have considerable potential for protecting archaeological sites (e.g. river valleys, marginal uplands and areas of blanket bogland). The designation affords some control over farming practices, peat extraction, forestry, tourism, industry and building. NHAs, however, are still only 'proposed designations' rather than designations in law. As it stands, proposed NHAs are afforded little protection; at Derryvicrone Bog, Connemara, for example, permission was given to plant despite objections from the National Parks and Wildlife Service (Hickie 1990, 3). The Forest Service, however, will not grant aid afforestation in NHAs or in areas considered to be ecologically important and consults with the National Parks and Wildlife Service on such matters.

The significance of such areas for archaeology lies in their potential ability to protect sites within their boundaries from development such as afforestation. There are, however, no management plans for the individual designated areas and therefore the effectiveness of the scheme may be limited.

Rural Environmental Protection Scheme (REPS)
REPS is the first farming scheme specifically designed to encourage 'environment friendly' farming. Most applicants to the scheme will employ an advisor to ensure eligibility for the scheme. The advisors are obliged to identify any recorded archaeological sites within the area. Any archaeology present on a farm must be actively protected from all potentially damaging farming activity. In many cases, this will not affect the

Implemented in May 1994, (under Council Regulation (EEC) No. 2078/92 as part of the CAP reforms), REPS developed from the 1992 Agri-Environment Programme. It was worth approximately £230 million to Ireland up to 1997, 75% of which was funded by the European Union. The main objective is to promote 'environmentally friendly' farming practices by reducing stock rates on farms, limiting the use of fertilisers and chemicals and improving water quality in rural areas. Although the initial take-up rate was low, the number of participating farmers has gradually increased to the point where funding is under severe pressure. The success of the scheme is reflected in recent criticism by Coillte's General Operations manager who identified REPS as being the main factor in the recent fall in

current farming practices, but some sites may have to be actively managed. The REP scheme has become increasingly popular, to the point of being considered responsible for the recent down-turn in afforestation figures. While the intentions of REPS are well-founded, the provision for archaeological protection is unenforceable. Archaeological assessment is only undertaken in exceptional cases and the majority of sites are never inspected.

planting rates (*Irish Farmers Journal,* January 24th, 1998). There are now over 200,000 hectares of land being farmed under the REP scheme, with the highest up-take in counties Galway, Cork and Tipperary.

The scheme is run over five years and can be worth up to £5,000 to an individual farmer. In addition, a participating farmer who has a proposed Natural Heritage Area on his/her land receives about £25 per hectare (£10 per acre) in addition to the REPS payment. To receive this fillip payment the farmer must ensure that specific environmental conditions are maintained. In exceptional cases the area proposed for designation (as NHA, SPA or SAC) may be so sensitive as to preclude farming activities, but in the majority of cases some modification to the current farming practices suffices. These areas are frequently in marginal land and therefore are threatened mainly by drainage, reclamation and afforestation.

Protection of archaeological/historical features is a mandatory condition of the scheme. Under 'Measure 7' of the scheme (Protection of features of historical and archaeological interest), the National Monuments Acts (1930 to 1994) are reinforced in practice. An archaeological monument occurring on a participating farm 'shall not be interfered with' and fencing around the monument/site is encouraged where necessary (for example, when carrying out activities involving heavy machinery). Afforestation, land reclamation, deep ploughing or removal of field boundaries are not permitted 'within those areas defined on the SMR' (D/AFF 1992, 36). In general, however, the REP scheme is only effective in protecting recorded sites.

Most applicants engage the services of an advisor to compile the necessary information required to join the scheme. In drawing up plans for applicants, an advisor is obliged to ensure that any known archaeological sites are protected. These advisors have an essential role in protecting and promoting archaeological sites, especially those which have not previously been recorded. Pre-bog walls and a stone enclosure, for example, were recently identified by a Teagasc officer in the course of planning an application for the REP scheme. The applicant had intended planting the area, unaware of the significance of the stone structures which were not previously recorded in any form and therefore not included in the SMR. As is frequently the case, the protection of these features relied not on specific regulations or legislation, but on an individual who was both interested and concerned about archaeology. Further co-operation and consultation between REPS advisors and archaeological authorities would undoubtedly produce similar results.

Despite limitations to the scheme, it has potential for protecting archaeology and for promoting awareness of archaeology in general. A similar scheme in Britain, the Environmentally Sensitive Areas Scheme, has already proven important for integrating archaeology into farm management (Macinnes 1993, 245). To realise the potential, a system of ensuring compliance with the regulations will have to be developed.

Landscape Alliance Ireland

Landscape Alliance Ireland was established in 1994 in response to increasing concern about the nature and management of the Irish landscape. It is a broad-based amalgamation of representatives from many sectors concerned about the landscape, including both archaeology and forestry. The primary objective of the organisation is to promote the introduction of a national landscape policy through discussion and debate, facilitated by its annual Landscape Forum (O'Regan 1996; 1997). In 1994, the organisation submitted a proposal document to government for a landscape policy which included heritage issues (O'Regan 1994). Given that archaeology is an integral part of the landscape, it must play a significant role in encouraging and formulating any such policy. The interaction between archaeology and other landscape issues (such as forestry) will undoubtedly benefit from exposure within the forum.

Forestry for Community
FFC are a pressure group whose concerns include the effect of afforestation on archaeology in rural areas.

Forestry for Community is a pressure group established, in 1987, in response to the increasing afforestation in the Cork/Kerry border region. The group now has considerable support nation-wide from a variety of people involved in rural issues. While the group's primary concerns centre on the effects of afforestation on rural communities and the environment, they have also highlighted the dangers to archaeological and historical features. Forestry for Community lobbies for management plans to be formulated with associated community, environmental and archaeological representatives. Their effectiveness is evident by the fact that the Forest Service in the Southwest region regard the group as a 'watch dog' and as a constant source of pressure to which they are answerable. Their significance for archaeology is two fold; first, in citing archaeology as a concern and second, raising awareness of heritage issues amongst the public. Similar concerns have been echoed by groups such as the Slieve Bloom Development Co-operative which also promotes sensitive planting, local community issues, and environmental and archaeological issues.

Crann

Crann is a voluntary organisation which promotes broadleaf planting in Ireland for social, environmental and educational aims. Given that a wooded landscape can be an appropriate setting for early prehistoric sites, there is great potential for promoting and developing mutually beneficial schemes through contact and co-operation with such an organisation.

The Tree Council of Ireland

The Tree Council of Ireland is a voluntary organisation which promotes educational and social activities within forestry and is also active in forestry research. It is, for example, the co-ordinating body for the annual National Tree Week. The organisation has also embarked on a research project at Balrath, Co. Meath, where it has leased 21 hectares of broadleaf woodland from Coillte (*Irish Farmers Journal*, April 29th, 1995). The aim of the project is to manage the woodland by emphasising silviculture, education and the recreational value of woodlands.

The involvement of organisations such as the Tree Council of Ireland and Crann is essential to the promotion of forests as environmental, cultural and leisure features of the Irish countryside. The increasing awareness of the social, cultural and tourist significance of woodlands is evident elsewhere in, for example, the allocation of National Lottery Funds in Britain to the Woodland Trust, an organisation established to promote education, enjoyment and appreciation of trees. In Ireland, Crann works towards similar aims. While the work carried out by these organisations is of essential environmental value, there is a need for closer contact between such organisations and archaeologists. It has to be stressed that regardless of the tree species, or the reason for planting, the potential threat to archaeology is the same.

Archaeology and the Forest Cycle

ARCHAEOLOGY IN FORESTRY
Evidence from Ireland and from abroad has demonstrated the potential impact of forestry on archaeology. The countrywide survey of known sites and monuments has only been in operation over the past two decades. It is not possible, therefore, to estimate the amount of archaeology already damaged or destroyed by forestry. In addition, a large proportion of sites are unrecorded and many will be destroyed without any record of their existence.

Archaeological sites and monuments in forestry, recorded and unrecorded, can be affected at all stages. The forest cycle involves processes common to arable farming such as ground preparation and harvesting. As with all agriculture, the effects depend on both the location and the intensity of the activity. The impact of tree planting, however, is more invasive than most traditional agricultural practices; the life cycle of the forest is considerably longer than other crops, the root network is extensive, and the tree canopy completely masks the area rendering site detection and inspection extremely difficult. Unlike other agricultural crops, forestry is a long-term development with a life cycle of roughly 30-35 years, in the case of coniferous plantations, and 70-100 years for broadleaf woodlands. Given the length of time involved, the potentially destructive nature of the tree root system, and the masking effect of the tree canopy, it follows that archaeology should be identified and protected before planting occurs. Where it is not identified and given adequate protection, any archaeological sites beneath or within the plantation may be damaged or destroyed. Sites which already exist within forestry require assessment and, where necessary, management.

It is not possible to estimate how much archaeology has been destroyed by afforestation but documented examples, such as those given by Foley *et al.* (1991) and IAPA (1994), provide indicators of the potential scale of destruction. Most of these examples were caused by State planting from the 1950s through to the early 1990s, before protective guidelines were introduced. Since the introduction of Forest Service guidelines on archaeology, the situation with respect to known sites in recently planted, semi-State forestry has improved considerably. There is still, however, a constant threat to sites, particularly to those which have not been recorded previously. Regardless of legal and practical protection, only a portion of sub-soil archaeology will ever be identified and much will be destroyed eventually by natural or human processes. It is essential, therefore, that the maximum amount of evidence is recovered before development. Afforestation rates in Ireland are no longer dominated by the semi-State sector and as the number of individuals and private companies involved increases annually, the need for controls to protect archaeology becomes more urgent.

THE PLANTING PROCESS

Land is prepared for planting by mounding, ripping, ploughing or pitting, depending on the soil type, terrain and species to be planted. Since archaeological remains are rarely buried at any great depth in the soil, each technique is capable of disturbing any deposits present. In some cases the damage will be minimal, especially where sites are recognised early in the process. In other cases, they will go unnoticed and will suffer from subsequent forestry processes.

Ground preparation
Planting preparation (Mounding, ripping and ploughing) will disturb any archaeology underground. While some techniques are less intrusive than others, they all

Mounding: The most common form of planting nowadays is referred to as 'mounding', where soil is dug out of a trench and piled up (*c.* 0.2m high) at regular intervals on the planting surface. The work is normally carried out by a machine which digs and sets the mounds. The mound provides an

involve a varying degree of subsoil disturbance. In addition, the use of heavy machinery poses a constant and serious threat to monuments in the vicinity.

aerated bed for the sapling and gives it a head start on the surrounding vegetation. Mounding has largely replaced deep ploughing as the primary planting technique and is used across a variety of soil types, but especially on gleys and peaty gleys (Bulfin 1992, 60). This method is probably the least invasive planting technique since it mainly involves removal of the topsoil. In poor-draining soils, however, the trench from which the mounds are dug is deepened to provide better drainage. Generally, mounding is avoided in better-quality soils where the drainage is adequate. The majority of better-quality sites will therefore be ripped, ploughed or planted directly. Recent research in ploughing equipment has also investigated machinery which combines more than one preparation technique, for example, the 'MacLarty mounder' fitted with equipment to mound and rip the soil simultaneously (*Irish Farmers Journal*, Oct. 21st, 1995). It is thought that this type of machine will be used commonly on mineral soils (*ibid.*).

Ripping: Where the natural drainage is impeded by a subsurface impermeable layer (iron panning for example), a technique known as 'ripping' is employed. A plough blade slices through the subsoil, breaking up the iron layer and mixing it with the topsoil. It is massively invasive and disturbs any subsurface archaeological material.

Ploughing ('tunnel' and 'double mouldboard'): Until the 1950s, blanket bogland was considered to be economically unviable for planting. The development of more advanced techniques of planting and deep ploughing equipment eventually allowed for ploughing on most soil types (Fig. 14). Nowadays ploughing is less common, but deep, invasive ploughing is still required on heavier boglands to maximise growth potential. The more usual form, double mouldboard ploughing, involves turning a broad central furrow, the upcast on both sides of which is used as the planting surface with the deep plough furrow acting as a drain (Bulfin 1992, 59). This method was the most common form of planting until recently and many of the mature forests in Ireland were established in such a manner. Consequently, archaeology beneath those forests was probably severely damaged even prior to subsequent root establishment.

Pit Planting: 'Pit' planting is usually employed for the more sensitive deciduous trees, particularly those planted for amenity purposes (Byrnes 1992, 4).

While most of the planting techniques will interfere with subsurface archaeology, they can also damage archaeology above ground level if it is not recognised before work begins. Heavy machinery is involved in most of the processes and, particularly on the softer soils, can cause considerable damage.

Drainage
Where the natural soil drainage is inadequate, extensive networks of drains are required. Archaeological remains are frequently disturbed or destroyed by these trenches and the damaged remains can often be seen in drain sections. In wetlands, organic remains frequently survive intact for thousands of years. When these lands are drained, the

On wet soils, such as low-lying swampy areas or blanket peatland and moors, preparation normally requires drainage of the land before ploughing. Where there is a risk to nearby streams, rivers or lakes, 'silt traps' are constructed to avoid siltation of the water systems. These are normally dug at the end of the drainage system and involve mechanical excavation deep into the subsoil.

Digging of drains and silt traps can in itself damage archaeological sites. The burnt material from a *fulacht fiadh* at Knocknakilla, Co. Cork, for

protective anaerobic conditions are lost and the decaying process is accelerated. Historic Scotland suggests that drainage trenches should be kept at least 30m from all known archaeological sites.

Maturity
Once trees have been planted, the subsequent threats to archaeology come from a variety of sources including changes in the water table, root systems, overgrowth of vegetation and wind-fall. In mature forestry the extent of these threats will depend on many factors — initial mitigation, location, soil type, management, etc. Closely set mature forestry often prevents access to, or identification of, archaeological sites.

example, was exposed in the section of a drainage trench and was not noticed until (incidental) archaeological inspection of the area took place. Similarly, it was noted that at least three of the seventeen *fulachta fiadh* recorded within forestry in Mid-Cork had been damaged by forestry-related drainage trenches.

Adequate drainage is essential to facilitate maximum growth-potential, and to ensure a water-free soil surface by directing sub-soil water away from the plantation. Extensive and effective drainage will, however, lead to the loss of protective anaerobic conditions for any organic archaeological traces in wetlands. Drainage systems, measuring over one metre in depth, can run throughout a plantation.

The Scottish archaeological authority, Historic Scotland, suggests that where drainage trenches are necessary, they should be kept at least 30m away from archaeological sites to avoid drying out of the protective anaerobic conditions (Barclay 1992, 43). On better-quality soils, with free drainage, this aspect of planting preparation will obviously be less intrusive.

Once an area has been ploughed and planted, existing archaeology faces threats from a wide range of factors, including the level of the water table, overgrowth of vegetation and wind-fall from the maturing trees. The combined effects of drainage and planting heighten the threat to archaeology — in the early stages of the forest cycle when there will normally be increased water run-off, and in the later stages as the forestry matures and water levels decrease with subsequent drying out of the soil (O'Halloran and Giller 1993, 42).

Fig. 14. *Knockadigeen hillfort, Co. Tipperary. The hill has been ploughed for forestry (Tom Condit).*

Despite initial protective measures, the unplanted 'buffer zone' around a monument and access to it will not remain free of vegetation for long. Natural regeneration of trees and shrubs will pose a threat to the monument and therefore need to be retarded. A typical Sitka spruce plantation reaches optimum maturity between 35 and 50 years and it is therefore essential that access to any monument within forestry be maintained to allow the condition of the site to be assessed when required. Throughout the forest cycle there is also a risk of damage to archaeological monuments caused by wind-throw. Damaged trees in the vicinity of a monument pose a danger to an upstanding monument.

An additional problem at this point is the identification of unrecorded sites and inspection of known or potential sites. The archaeological inventories for West and Mid Cork (Power 1992; 1997), for example, report that of 195 sites recorded as being within forestry, 26 were inaccessible due to dense planting. Where an area has not been surveyed previously, mature forestry renders site detection extremely difficult, if not impossible. It is not possible, for example, to identify most sites in forestry through aerial reconnaissance. As the tree canopy develops, the opportunity to detect sites diminishes; closely set trees obliterate all visible traces of archaeology from the air. Coupled with the difficulty of passage within a commercial forest, detecting unrecorded sites in mature forestry is unlikely to be possible.

Root systems
The extensive root network will damage any archaeological site or feature beneath the soil.

Regardless of the scale of the operation, planting is potentially damaging or destructive to any existing archaeological features. Where trees are planted solely for commercial purposes, obviously there will be a tendency to optimise the number of trees per acre. Trees in early State plantations tended to be closely set (*c.* 1.4m apart), but the normal spacing is now about two metres apart for coniferous trees. Planted at this distance, a hectare of land will sustain as many as 2,500 trees (or *c.* 1,000 trees per acre) (Bulfin 1992, 67). To promote more regular stem growth, broadleaves are normally planted at a slightly closer distance to each other, that is, *c.* 1.8m apart. Plantations will, therefore, have an extensive root network, and it is estimated that 'a large tree can be in contact with up to 4,500 cubic metres (around 10,000 tons) of soil' (*ibid.*, 27). The roots can penetrate even the smallest soil particle and will, consequently, invade any buried archaeological deposits encountered. On peaty soils the root spread will be even more extensive as the roots attempt to secure anchorage against the wind. Subsoil sites escaping destruction in the ground preparation stage may still suffer damage from the root network. Many broadleaf species, because of their deep rooting system, are potentially even more damaging than their coniferous counterparts.

Harvesting and thinning
Tree-felling and the large machinery involved in extraction activities can obviously cause structural damage to existing sites in forestry. While the required buffer zone should afford some protection, this has not always been the case. The unplanted area must not be used for dumping of material or for parking of machinery. Sites should be clearly marked out on the ground with stakes, and cordoned off where necessary.

Once improvement, pruning and thinning of a plantation begins (between 17 and 25 years) there is an increased risk of damage to archaeology in the area. Thinning is carried out, either mechanically or using chainsaws, to remove some of the trees or branches to allow the remaining crop to reach optimum cropping size. It generates a considerable amount of waste and normally encourages natural regeneration of vegetation on the forest floor. Archaeological sites within the plantation should therefore be monitored, or at least clearly marked out, at this stage to ensure their safety.

The felling of trees (including thinning and harvesting) is licensed under the 1946 Forestry Act, but control of felling relates primarily to silvicultural issues. The Strategic Plan for the Development of the Forestry Sector in Ireland is particularly concerned about this aspect of the forestry sector.

> *'The limitations of the existing forestry legislation in relation to environmental issues, its cumbersome procedures and the lack of comprehensive guidelines covering felling and extraction are potential obstacles to effective management and control in this area.' (D/AFF 1996, 36, 4.3.21).*

The Plan notes, however, that new guidelines are being prepared to address the situation (*ibid*. 38, 4.3.31) and advises a review of the Act to allow issues such as amenity and the environment to be considered (*ibid*. 78, 4.17.7).

An additional risk during the thinning and felling stage is that the protective buffer zone around a monument may serve as a temporary dump (Barclay 1992, 41). Given the lack of archaeological supervision in the field, it is essential that sites should be demarcated to minimise the risk of damage. This is particularly important when dealing with low-visibility sites or sites whose full extent may not be obvious to the untrained eye. Standardised and clearly visible stakes should be used to identify the site and the site should be cordoned off, if necessary, during periods of forestry activity. An alternative and more attractive approach has been taken in the Snowdonia National Park where marking of sites is done by planting broadleaf trees, at a safe distance, around appropriate monuments (Lee 1995, 103). The advantage to such an approach is that the maturing broadleaf trees will stand out against the conifers, clearly identifying the area as being of significance, while adding diversity to the forest environment.

Commercial plantations are normally clear-felled and large and heavy machinery is used to carry out the process. Lee (*ibid*., 98) reports that the most damaging operations carried out in the forests of the North York Moors National Park involved the 'movement of vehicles and equipment and the extraction of timber, especially when the latter is performed by skidding (chain-dragging trunks behind a tractor)'. Considerable attention must be paid to archaeological sites at this stage in the forest cycle. While this is pointed out in the Forest Service guidelines and by Coillte's policy on archaeology, it is not possible to monitor the situation in practice. It is especially difficult to enforce such a guideline when contract workers are employed with the added possibility of standards not being maintained.

One of the side effects of clear-felling large areas is the potentially detrimental soil disturbance and sediment removal. Although more advanced equipment and new techniques are minimising these effects, the environmental dangers from flash floods or excessive soil slippage are often addressed by drainage systems which may intensify the damage to subsoil archaeology in the immediate or surrounding area.

Removing trees from archaeological sites
When a site has already been planted, the question arises whether to remove the trees or to allow them remain in situ. Where the root system has not yet fully established, the trees and their roots should be removed, particularly where mound-planting has been used. If the trees are mature, however, removal of the tree stump and roots will cause considerable damage to any sub-soil archaeology. In such a case, the trees should be felled with the stump left in place.

Where an archaeological site is already planted, damage limitation comes into effect. The damage caused by trees will obviously vary from one site to another and depends on site type, tree species, planting method and extraction techniques. An example at Castleblagh, Co. Cork demonstrates how consultation between the forestry and archaeologists can result in mutually acceptable courses of action that attempt to minimise the impact on archaeological sites. Coillte (South-Western Region) consulted the Department of Archaeology, UCC, regarding extraction of mature trees from a large earthen enclosure in North Cork (SMR no. CO034-046). The Environmental Officer was willing to leave the valuable stand of Norway spruce remain *in situ* if extraction would cause additional damage to the enclosure. After field inspection and discussion with the Environmental Officer, a decision was taken to hand-fell the trees using a 'staking' technique and to remove the timber through one agreed area of the site (see Appendix 1, for additional details). The enclosure at Castleblagh was in mature forestry and therefore extraction of the roots/stumps was not recommended. Recently planted sites, however, might have the trees removed with minimal damage. Such a course of action was recommended, for example, at Kilbronoge, Co. Cork where a wedge tomb (SMR no. CO140-042) was planted in 1995 with oak saplings. In this case, removal of the trees would obviously cause less damage than allowing them to mature. A similar course of action was recommended for two *fulachta fiadh* in Co. Cork, both of which had been planted recently, although one had been included in the SMR (CO016-147).

Although equipment is available nowadays for extracting trees in sensitive environments, sophisticated techniques are not always necessary. Consultation with archaeologists prior to removal of the trees, however, is essential to ensure that the risk of damage is minimised.

Reforestation
Much State forestry is now reaching maturity and almost half of Coillte's recent planting has been reforestation of these areas. This presents an opportunity to survey areas that have been under trees for the past four or five decades. Many of these areas are remote upland and marginal areas where archaeological sites might be expected to exist. Areas which have been recently harvested should be surveyed before reforestation.

The Strategic Plan for forestry recommends that the productive forest estate should be maintained by reforestation following clear-felling (D/AFF 1996, 30, 4.1.27). In 1994, over 50% of Coillte's planting was reforestation (see Fig. 15), reflecting the fact that early State forestry is now reaching maturity and will be extracted over the next few years. Between 1989 and 1996, Coillte reforested almost 29,000 hectares of land (Tithe an Oireachtais 1997, 62).

This rate of harvesting and reforestation presents archaeology with a number of positive opportunities: a) to remove trees which are planted on or too close to archaeological sites; b) to ensure that existing sites are not replanted and c) to investigate areas which have been under dense forestry for the past four or five decades. Provision must be made, in relation to the latter point (c), to allow archaeological surveys of selected areas before reforestation. Since a harvested area is normally left unplanted for at least one year before reforestation, it provides an opportunity to survey the area in an attempt to minimise any further damage to archaeological sites. Such a programme of 'archaeological sampling' was carried out along the River Bann drainage dumps, in counties Antrim and Down, between the felling of a mature plantation and replanting of the areas (Bourke 1995, 7, no. 9). In the case of one site, Gortgole, Co. Antrim, a range of artefacts from the Mesolithic to the Hiberno-Norse period was recovered (Bourke 1996, 2, no. 5).

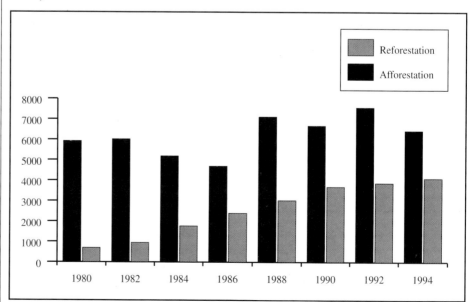

Fig. 15. *State Afforestation and Reforestation. Many early State-planted forests are now reaching maturity and will be felled over the next few years.*

While the protection of known archaeological sites should now be regarded as standard practice, the potential for identifying archaeological sites after clear-felling is a more ambitious endeavour. Areas which have been clear-felled are normally littered with timber debris which will obscure all but the most obvious feature (Fig. 16). It is questionable whether or not any archaeological features could be detected in such an area. There is, however, some evidence from abroad to suggest that sites can still be identified after harvesting and before the land is replanted. The survey of the forested area of the North York Moors National Park (Lee 1995), for example, discovered that many sites which were thought to have been destroyed by earlier planting had actually survived 'albeit planted over with trees' (*ibid.*, 98). Since much of the planting had been carried out by hand, the damage caused to archaeological sites was less than had been anticipated. The worst structural damage had actually been caused by forest tracks and by ploughing.

Forest roads
Forest roads are exempt from all planning laws.

Given the remote location of many plantations, it follows that the majority of developments will require substantial routes to allow access for machinery. Between 1992-93, for example, Coillte constructed over 229km of forest roads (Coillte Teoranta 1994). The government forecast that 1,400km of forest roads will have been constructed or upgraded through grant assistance by the year 2000 (D/AFF 1994a, 141). While planning permission is required for most road construction, forest roads are generally exempt from the requirements.

Under normal circumstances forest roads are not required until the first thinnings are taken (10-15 years), but access routes are required for the initial planting, particularly where extensive drainage systems are to be constructed. Since the land is frequently wet, further drainage systems are put in place to protect the roads, adding to the invasive digging process.

Fig. 16. *Carn Tigernagh, Fermoy, Co. Cork after clear felling (Gina Johnson).*

Fires breaks/rides
While forest fires are not common in Ireland, they do occur and as planting increases, so too does the need to ensure that sites in forestry are protected. Well-planned fire breaks offer the potential for ensuring continued access to some archaeological sites within the forest.

Forest fires, although relatively uncommon in Ireland, are nonetheless a threat to archaeology within a plantation. Coillte's company report for 1994 reported a total of 272 hectares (672 acres) destroyed by fire. While there are no reports available of damage to archaeological sites, it reinforces the need to maintain the area immediately around the site free of trees and overgrowth.

To contain any fire that might occur, fire breaks are established at planting stage. Although these have a primary functional purpose, they could also be planned to facilitate access to existing sites in forestry. Macinnes (1993, 247) suggests that 'archaeological features can be incorporated into forest plantations as open spaces for fire breaks...and should be accessible from forest rides for ease of management'. Planning in the establishment stage of a plantation would ensure that access to an archaeological site is maintained by running a fire-belt close to the site. This is not unreasonable given that the Forest Service suggests that fire-belts should 'follow an irregular route' and 'should not be sited at right angles or parallel to contours' in the landscape (Forest Service b).

MANAGEMENT OF ARCHAEOLOGY IN FORESTRY

Ideally, archaeological sites in forestry should be visited at regular intervals to ensure that they are accessible, maintained free of vegetation and undamaged. There are no management strategies nor guidelines in place for such procedures. This is a situation which must be addressed through a co-operative and integrated approach between archaeologists, foresters and environmentalists.

Identifying sites and legally protecting them are fundamental aspects of the management process. Ensuring continued protection of those sites is also essential but conserving, exploiting and excavating must all be considered as options for managing sites within forestry (Darvill 1986, 39). The variety of archaeological sites and their locations in Ireland are so diverse that a range of different approaches is required. Ideally, management schemes would be prescribed for individual sites, taking the site and local conditions into consideration. Such a detailed planning process cannot be achieved at present and therefore a more general scheme is in operation. As a result, protection of archaeology, in practice, tends to deal primarily with the visible aspect of known sites (protected by the National Monuments Acts).

An example from the townland of Ballygrady North, Co. Cork, demonstrates how even the protection of SMR sites is not always achieved in practice. An area of deciduous planting involved two known archaeological sites, both recorded in the SMR. The planting respected an obvious burial ground (SMR no. CO016-146) and was kept at the required distance from the boundary of the site. A low mound, identified by the SMR as a *fulacht fiadh* (SMR no. CO016-147) was evidently not recognised by those carrying out the planting and has young oak saplings planted into it (Cork Archaeological Survey, pers. comm.). This incident reinforces the need for archaeological inspection of planting operations; it also indicates the general tendency to recognise only the highly visible aspects of archaeology. Cooney (1991, 70-71) warns that the focus on major sites and impressive site-types tends to distract from other equally important, although less obvious, sites.

Inventory of sites in forestry
There is no inventory of archaeological sites in forests. It is not possible, therefore, to formulate effective management policies and schemes.

The first step to effective protection and management of archaeological sites in forestry is identifying which sites already exist within forests. At present, the Forest Service is re-mapping all forestry in Ireland. When that survey is complete, an amalgamation of the results with SMR/Record of Monuments and Places and Inventory information would provide a list of all known sites and monuments in forests. This would allow particularly sensitive sites or those known to be in danger to be assessed. While the preliminary status of SMRs and Records of Monuments and Places is acknowledged, such a listing would also act as a basis for formulating management strategies for archaeological sites in forestry.

***Classifying sites for
management purposes***
*It is not practically possible to
manage the estimated 150,000
to 200,000 known pre-1700
AD sites as individual entities.
Some sites will require more
active management than
others. A system of evaluating
and quantifying sites for the
purposes of management may
have to be developed.*

At present, all sites included in the Register of Historic Monuments and in the Record of Monuments and Places are legally protected from unauthorised interference. The system designates equal status to each site, so that a partially damaged monument is afforded the same legal protection as an intact monument. Given that complete field surveys of most sites have yet to be carried out, it is important that the status quo should persist. Ultimately, however, a system of evaluation or quantification will be required to allow for practical management of archaeological sites under threat from developments such as afforestation. A system of classifying sites according to a defined set of criteria already operates in Britain. Survival/condition, period, rarity, fragility/vulnerability, diversity, documentation, group value and potential are the main criteria identified by English Heritage for evaluating ancient monuments (e.g. Lambrick 1992; Breeze 1993). While such classifications are valuable management tools for individual sites, their suitability for formulating overall management policy is debatable. Pre-defining criteria for 'evaluating' archaeological sites can involve biased and transitory cultural values that may prove to be detrimental to the archaeological record. Carver (1996, 45) suggests that the archaeological resource should be viewed 'primarily as a research 'asset' in the form of deposits rather than monuments' and that a symbiotic relationship can be achieved between development and management of the archaeological resource. In the case of afforestation, the sites most likely to be protected from the development are upstanding monuments.

Fig. 17. *The court tomb at Magheranrush, Co. Sligo has been completely surrounded by dense forestry, removing the site from its wider context (Ordnance Survey).*

***Landscape setting of
monuments***
*Archaeological monuments
sometimes occur in groups or
form a significant element of
the landscape. The visual
impact of forestry on such
monuments should be
considered pre-afforestation.*

There is also a tendency to emphasise individual sites while the broader question of prehistoric landscapes and the landscape context of monuments is not addressed. Although the legislation allows for places of archaeological potential to be included in the Record of Monuments and Places, the Forest Service guidelines do not mention the landscape context of monuments or the possibility of land containing groups of associated sites or monuments. In Britain, the Forestry Commission guidelines (*ibid.*) promote the idea of preserving the setting of sites that are in dominant landscape positions, for example, a megalithic tomb in a prominent position on a hillside. The visual impact of forestry on the setting of a monument can be significant in terms of appreciation and promotion of archaeology. It is an aspect that must be considered in assessing the overall impact of afforestation (Fig. 17).

Groups of sites, sites that are inter-visible, or extensive sites can form part of a prehistoric or historic landscape. Structures such as stone circles, standing stones and stone alignments, for example, sometimes occur in close proximity to each other and their associated setting should be preserved with unplanted areas between them. In other cases, monuments stretch for considerable distances, often forming an integral part of the landscape (Fig. 18). Pre-bog field walls, for example, can stretch across an expanse of land and preservation orders might be merited in some cases to prevent any planting. In the majority of cases, however, considerate planning of forestry can accommodate archaeological features and their settings. As Cooney (1993, 19) points out, a woodland setting may be more appropriate for many early prehistoric monuments than the current modified surroundings in which they exist.

Co-operative management
In woodlands primarily intended for recreation and/or environmental purposes, archaeology can be a beneficial aspect. Archaeological sites within forestry can enhance the forest environment and provide additional attractions, particularly in Forest Parks and trails.

When co-operative management schemes are in place, archaeology and forestry are not incompatible aspects of the landscape. This is particularly true of forests and woodlands whose primary functions are for leisure, recreational and educational activities and which are of environmental and ecological benefit. In these woodlands, management systems can be implemented not just to protect archaeology but to promote and enhance sites within the forest environment. Archaeology adds diversity and provides an additional attraction for visitors pursuing leisure or sporting activities.

Fig. 18. *The hillfort at Formoyle, Co. Clare is a dominant landscape monument, but forestry has been allowed to intrude to the rampart of the site (Tom Condit).*

A symbiotic relationship is more difficult to achieve in commercial plantations where financial considerations are obviously a priority. While there is legislation in place to protect archaeological sites, there are no laws regarding management of the same sites. The Forest Service and Coillte

Teoranta have policies and guidelines in place to protect archaeology during the planting process. They do not, however, have a management policy for archaeology within the maturing forests. Once a forest has been established the level of management is low-key until the thinning process begins, about 10-15 years later. During this time any archaeology present may be engulfed by vegetation that will flourish in the initial stages of the forest cycle. It is therefore important that access to the site be maintained to ensure that no lasting damage is caused. There are, however, no provisions made for archaeologists to visit sites in forestry, and there is no requirement of the land-owner to maintain the sites free of overgrowth.

In contrast, the Forestry Commission in Scotland consults the archaeological authorities on the maintenance of sites and they control excess vegetation growth in and around sites, where necessary, as part of the forest management scheme. Management of the sites is facilitated by the presence of Regional Archaeologists. Specific management schemes are proscribed for particularly sensitive monuments, or where a site is considered to be under threat and some financial assistance is available for essential maintenance and management (Breeze 1993, 49).

Environmental considerations
Co-operative management requires equal status for environmental, ecological and archaeological concerns.

Co-operative management of archaeological sites in forestry incorporates other issues such as the environmental or ecological aspects of the immediate area. Complex situations which also involve environmental and landscape considerations have to be dealt with in an inclusive manner (Yarnell 1993, 29). An area where archaeological concerns might conflict with environmental issues is the case of vegetation overgrowth on a site within forestry. From an ecological perspective, allowing natural regeneration of clearings within a forest is desirable, allowing for greater wildlife diversity. From an archaeological perspective, however, such regeneration can be as threatening as if the site had been planted in the first place. This is an issue which requires considerable co-operation between all sectors involved. In many cases, archaeological sites will have to be given priority since they are non-renewable resources. Compromises can, however, be reached with appropriate management schemes in place. A mutually beneficial option, for example, might be to plant broadleaf trees at the edge of the buffer zone as is done in the Snowdonia National Park (Lee 1995, 103).

CHAPTER 5

Archaeology and Forestry in the United Kingdom

INTRODUCTION
Over the past decade, Northern Ireland, Scotland and Wales have experienced a similar afforestation programme to that in Ireland. There are additional guidelines and different methods of enforcement in the three countries. The systems involved are outlined here for comparison with the Republic of Ireland.

The Forestry Commission
The Forestry Commission is the State agency responsible for developing forestry in the United Kingdom. The basic policy with regard to protection of archaeology is similar to that of the Irish Forest Service. To qualify for European planting grants, Forestry Commission guidelines on archaeology must be respected.

Approximately 10% of the United Kingdom is under forestry, a figure comparable with Ireland's 8% and equally low in the European context. Unlike the Republic of Ireland, however, Britain has a less extensive planting programme — the average planting rate up to 1994 was only *c.* 15,000 hectares annually compared with the Republic's almost 17,000 hectares. The British planting programme has placed a heavy emphasis in recent years on the environment and on sporting and leisure activities; therefore, 55% of all new planting is of broadleaves compared with approximately 20% in Ireland. This priority is also reflected in the allocation of British Lottery funds to the Woodland Trust whose function is to promote woodlands for social, leisure and educational activities.

The Forestry Commission is the British counterpart of the Irish Forest Service and is responsible for State planting and the administration of forestry grants. It has overall responsibility for the development of forestry in Britain. Active management of State forestry is carried out by Forest Enterprise and grants are administered by The Forestry Authority. The basic policy of the Forestry Commission with regard to archaeology is similar to that of the Irish Forest Service, that is, 'sites of archaeological importance should be conserved' (Forestry Commission 1995, 1). The realisation that forestry activities are a major threat to archaeology led to the establishment of a variety of programmes designed to stem the extent of the damage. One such project, for example, was the North York Moors Forest Survey Project, initiated in 1992 as a joint endeavour between the archaeological and forestry authorities (Lee 1995). While a primary objective of the project was to identify and record archaeological sites in forestry, emphasis was also placed on developing management prescriptions for those sites (*ibid.*, 99). This focus on management is a progressive attitude towards archaeology in British forests which is facilitated through communication between the archaeological and forestry sectors.

The Forestry Commission specifies various environmental and archaeological standards that must be observed to qualify for the Woodland Grant Scheme (Forestry Commission 1995). The archaeological guidelines are similar to those of the Forest Service in Ireland, but they are more specific and include aspects that are not considered in the current Irish guidelines. It is recommended that an area of at least 20m should be left unplanted around most archaeological sites, and that drainage trenches should be at least 30m from the outermost perimeter of an archaeological site. The landscape context and the visibility of monuments is afforded considerable weight in the guidelines, and it is also suggested that where groups of archaeological features occur close together, they 'should be incorporated into a larger area of open space' (*ibid.*, 4). Private landowners and forestry companies are encouraged to allow ample open space between associated sites or groups of monuments. This effectively maintains the monuments' setting, at least in part, and where access is facilitated, provides an attractive and educational resource within the forest.

The Forestry Commission defines management of sites as including maintenance of existing grass or heather cover; removal of trees which may threaten a site (e.g. trees which are vulnerable to windthrow); controlling public access where a site is under threat and maintaining the 'visibility of [certain] monuments in a wider landscape' (*ibid.*, 5).

The distribution and nature of forests in the United Kingdom is very different to the Republic of Ireland. The most recent figures available show that 27% of UK forests are deciduous compared with 10% of Irish forests. In addition, while 57% of UK woodlands are in private ownership, about 20% of Irish woodlands are privately owned. England has approximately 7.3% of land under trees, but most commercial afforestation has been focused on Scotland (12.6% forest cover) and Wales (11.6%) (O'Halloran and Giller 1993, 36). This has focused on similar land types to Ireland, that is, uplands, marginal agricultural land and poor-grade moors (Lee 1995, 97). As a result, the archaeological authorities in Scotland and Wales have had to respond to a threat similar to that existing in Ireland. While the regulations for controlling afforestation are similar throughout the UK, their methods of implementation differ considerably.

NORTHERN IRELAND
The Department of Agriculture in Northern Ireland (DANI) is responsible for all state forestry and for the distribution of European Union and British government grants.

The history of forestry in Northern Ireland ran a similar course to that of the Republic before separation of the two jurisdictions in 1922. Since then, afforestation in the Republic has followed a different route, although in recent years there has been close contact between Northern Ireland and the Republic on forestry issues, facilitated by the Forestry Liaison Group (D/AFF 1994a, 180). There is additional contact in the form of Interreg, a European Union initiative which promotes development in forestry on both sides of the Irish border.

The Forest Service in Northern Ireland, operating under the Department of Agriculture (D/ANI), is responsible for State-owned forestry and carries out its own planting and management of forests.

Forestry policy
Forestry policy in Northern Ireland is broadly similar to that in the Republic of Ireland. Guidelines exist to protect environmental and archaeological features within forestry. As in the Republic, there is a shift away from marginal lands and onto better-quality lowlands.

In 1992, following the United Nations conference on the Environment and Development (the Earth Summit), forest policy, objectives, formats, restrictions and management of forestry in Northern Ireland were redefined (D/ANI 1993). A target planting rate was established to increase overall forest cover to 120,000 hectares (8.5% of the land) by the end of the century. As in the Republic, there has also been a shift in emphasis from encouraging afforestation on marginal, unenclosed land to promoting planting on better-quality enclosed lowlands. Guidelines were put in place to ensure sustainable land use and environmental and archaeological protection. As with the rest of Britain, there is a stated policy of developing multi-functional forestry, that is, forestry for recreation, conservation, education and for scenic benefits as well as for its economic value. The Forest Service (NI) manages forest nature reserves and National Nature Reserves where forestry is promoted for its conservation, recreation and amenity value (*ibid.*). In addition, it now operates a general policy of not planting blanket and raised bogland, undisturbed bogland and cut-over bog capable of natural regeneration (Tomlinson 1997, 132).

Protection of archaeology
Archaeology is protected under the Historic Monuments Acts. Co-operation between the Environment and Heritage

Where proposed planting occurs close to an Historic Monument, the application is referred to the Environment and Heritage Service (EHS) of the Department of the Environment for Northern Ireland (D/OENI). On aver-

Service and the forestry authorities provides additional protection for archaeology in State forests.

age the EHS is consulted on about 400 grant applications a year (C. Foley, pers. comm.). The Forest Service also consult the EHS prior to acquiring land. Where any significant effects on the environment or on the archaeology of an area are likely, an Environmental Impact Assessment is required (this is determined at the discretion of the Forest Service in consultation with the EHS). EIAs are mandatory for planting over 100 hectares but can be requested for any planting proposal which is likely to impact on the environment.

The EHS supplies each District Forest area with information (site location, description, etc.) on all known sites on their property. The guidelines for general protection of archaeology in forestry are similar to those in the Republic but there are some additional features. The EHS adds a general management prescription for each site within forestry (C. Foley, pers. comm.). Where a site is particularly fragile, for example, special instructions will be outlined to ensure that forestry activity doesn't interfere with or damage it. The EHS has asked that any such advice given be written into management plans for each forest to protect against developments in the future.

There is continuous formal and informal contact between foresters and archaeologists, and the general attitude of the Forest Service towards historical and archaeological sites appears to be very positive. This is reinforced by the Forest Service Conservation Committee which meets with interested sectors, including archaeologists, roughly six times a year. The committee's primary concerns are environmental and archaeological protection within forests. Afforestation which is not grant-aided is outside the scope of their brief but where possible private interests and companies involved in planting are contacted by archaeologists within the EHS.

SCOTLAND
The distribution of Scottish afforestation is similar to that occurring in Ireland. Uplands and marginal agricultural land have been the focus of afforestation but better-quality lowlands are increasingly being planted. The Scottish archaeological authorities have developed a close and progressive relationship with the forestry sector.

Since the 1950s, Britain has experienced unprecedented rates of planting, much of it located in Scotland. Eighty-six per cent of all new planting between 1975 and 1985, for example, was carried out in Scotland (Walker 1986, 116). The rise in afforestation continued through the early 1980s with no apparent regard for archaeological concerns. Although some pre-planting field surveys were carried out during the late 1970s and early 1980s (e.g. Mercer 1980), afforestation remained largely uncontrolled until the late 1980s. This situation arose largely because archaeology in Scotland has traditionally had a relatively close relationship with the public and with state bodies. When the Ancient Monuments and Archaeological Areas (AMAA) Act (1979) was introduced in Britain, for example, the arrangement between archaeologists and local authority planners was thought to be so secure in Scotland that there was no need to designate specific areas. Partially as a result of such informal arrangements, large-scale afforestation caused considerable damage to and destruction of archaeological sites. The response from the Scottish archaeological authorities is of particular interest to Ireland because of the similar planting trends. The archaeological infrastructure in Scotland, however, differs considerably from that in Ireland, particularly in its use of local-level field officers.

Indicative Forestry Strategies (IFSs)
The distribution of Scottish afforestation is largely determined by Indicative

The Forestry Commission was responsible for the formation of Indicative Forestry Strategies (IFSs). Scotland, which was the first European Union region to develop such strategies, introduced them in response to the

Forestry Strategies (IFSs), which were initiated by the Forestry Commission.

uncontrolled planting of the 1970s and early 1980s. They were implemented as policy frameworks for regional development within Indicative Regional Strategies (Goodstadt 1991). The first IFS was developed in the Strathclyde region where 28% of the region was under forestry by 1991. A GIS computer-based system was compiled to include major land, landscape, cultural and heritage issues. There is now a legal requirement for each Regional Council to have an IFS. The Scottish IFSs differ from the Irish IFS in the overall objective. Scottish systems identify areas suitable for afforestation by classifying land as 'preferred', 'potential' or 'sensitive' depending on its potential for supporting forestry (*ibid.*).

Historic Scotland
Historic Scotland is responsible for the 'built' heritage in Scotland. Its monument wardens inspect Scheduled Ancient Monuments (SAMs) at regular intervals to assess their condition within forestry.

Historic Scotland is responsible for the protection and promotion of scheduled ancient monuments. While it has the power to schedule any archaeological site, it is primarily concerned with protecting monuments of 'national importance'. Scheduled Ancient Monuments are inspected by Historic Scotland monument wardens once every few years to ensure preservation.

Historic Scotland also administers two grant schemes designed to encourage and facilitate the protection of archaeological sites and monuments: 1) 'Grants To Owners' (GTO) — available to assist in paying for any maintenance or repairs which might be required, and 2) 'Management Agreements' — which can be agreed with a landowner to pay for erection of protective fencing, removal of trees, control of grazing, etc. Historic Scotland is also involved in training foresters at the various universities and at the Scottish School of Forestry. In 1995, Historic Scotland issued a Statement of Intent as the basis of an agreement with Scottish Natural Heritage. They intend working together to co-operate on issues effecting 'natural, archaeological and historical aspects of the environment', for example, forestry. The co-operation is particularly concerned with designated areas such as Natural Heritage Areas and with formulating management schemes for these areas. They intend to develop an integrated approach to land-use management.

Regional and Island Areas Archaeologists
The Forestry Commission informs either the Regional Archaeologist or an Historic Scotland officer of all proposed planting. The Regional Archaeologists are normally the first point of contact for advice on archaeology in forestry. They play an essential and active role in ensuring protection and management of archaeology. Where necessary, the site is inspected and marked out on the ground by the archaeologist and all forestry activity must avoid the defined clearing.

Most regional councils in Scotland employ an archaeologist who normally operates within the planning department. Regional Archaeologists are involved in co-ordinating information on newly discovered sites for inclusion in the SMRs. They are responsible for dealing with archaeological aspects of the planning process and for providing information and advice to the public.

The Forestry Commission operates a notification system whereby all planting in an area must be reported to the archaeological authorities; Regional Archaeologists are normally the first point of contact in assessing all cases of proposed new planting (Barclay 1992, 35). A decision, based on SMR information and on the records of the local archaeologist, is taken as to whether a site visit is warranted or not. The results of the site inspection and/or assessment are then passed on to the Forestry Commission who communicate any prescribed management measures to the landowner. Where a single monument is involved, the grant applicant must undertake to protect the site by leaving a buffer zone of at least 20m from the edge of the site. Where large areas are to be planted and the evidence suggests high archaeological potential, a field survey is commissioned (*ibid.*, 36). When necessary, the Regional Archaeologist also liaises with the Forestry Commission regarding sites already in forestry. The primary advantage of local-level assessment of planting proposals is that sites can be inspected by an archaeologist prior to and/or during planting preparation where necessary. When a site is particularly fragile or the remains are not obvious, the archaeologist will physically mark out the limits of the site to identify it clearly on the ground. Barclay (*ibid.*, 36-37) argues that marking out of the site by a professional archaeologist is the most important part of the process of physically protecting sites.

Royal Commission on the Ancient and Historical Monuments of Scotland (RCAHMS)

The RCAHMS is responsible for maintaining and updating the National Monuments Record. It works largely in the form of two survey teams, one of which is the Afforestable Land Survey. The RCAHMS also has an aerial photography programme which concentrates on identifying lowland sites.

Of particular relevance to the current Irish situation is the type of land planted in Scotland. The areas most affected have been the upland and marginal agricultural areas, where vast tracks of forestry were planted without prior surveying or recording of archaeological sites. Vast tracts of blanket bog in the north of Scotland were heavily targeted by investors until the UK Government abolished the tax relief incentive for forestry in 1988 (Shepherd 1992, 163). A contemporary report commissioned by the British National Audit Office (PIEDA 1986) indicated that actual rates of return from planting blanket bogland were 'extremely low'. A combination of poor economic forecasts and pressure from environmental concerns led to the Forestry Commission's decision not to acquire further bogland that was considered to be of environmental or archaeological importance.

The Woodland Grant Scheme (WGS)
The Woodland Grant Scheme specifically requires protection of archaeology during all forestry activity. Historic Scotland Officers and Regional Archaeologists are essential in ensuring adherence to the scheme. The Forestry Commission notifies either the archaeological authorities (normally the Regional Archaeologist or Historic Scotland) of all new planting proposals.

Until 1988, the protection of archaeology during afforestation and in forestry had largely been at the discretion of the Forestry Commission — a situation not unlike that which exists in Ireland. The Forestry Commission submitted long-term plans to the archaeological authorities for assessment and informed them of any unrecorded sites recognised in the field. Landowners, however, were responsible for notifying the authorities of any monuments on the proposed area for planting. Barclay (1992, 35) points out that during this time of voluntary notification, not one unscheduled monument was reported to the archaeological authorities.

A significant growth in private sector planting throughout the 1980s led to a situation where the informal arrangement between Historic Scotland and the Forestry Commission was recognised as inadequate to deal with the amount of forestry activity. In 1987 the Royal Commission on the Ancient and Historical Monuments of Scotland estimated that up to 5,000 monuments could be destroyed through afforestation by the year 2000 (Shepherd 1992, 165). The Society of Antiquaries of Scotland lobbied MPs to establish regulations and funding for the protection of archaeology within areas to be forested. The government responded by introducing the 'Woodland Grant Scheme' (WGS) in 1988 which established formal systems for dealing with the protection of archaeology in areas to be afforested. The pressure on archaeology in afforestable areas led to the formation of the Afforestable Land Survey in the same year.

The introduction of the Woodland Grant Scheme (WGS) in 1989 saw the first formal protective measures for archaeological sites in forestry. Included in the scheme is the 'notification system' whereby the Forestry

Commission must notify the archaeological authorities of all planting proposals (both public and State). Initially, a centralised consultative archaeological system was considered but it was eventually agreed that the Regional Archaeologists would be the primary point of contact for the Forestry Commission. Significantly, two years after the introduction of the Woodland Grant Scheme a major forestry company had a six-figure grant withheld and was fined (under the AMAA Act) for causing damage to an archaeological site.

The Afforestable Land Survey (ALS)

In conjunction with the Forestry Commission, Historic Scotland and the Regional Archaeologist (or equivalent), the Afforestable Land Survey (ALS) of the RCAHMS identifies land that is likely to be afforested in the future and that is considered to be of high archaeological potential. Large areas of land are then surveyed and all sites in the area recorded for inclusion in the Sites and Monuments Record. The Forestry Commission is advised of the presence of sites, and areas of archaeological importance can then be excluded from the local Indicative Forestry Strategy.

The Afforestable Land Survey (of the Royal Commission on the Ancient and Historic Monuments of Scotland) was established in 1989 to deal specifically with archaeological sites in land that 'might be at risk from future afforestation throughout Scotland' (Halliday and Ritchie 1992, 169). Given that most commercial planting has taken place in upland and marginal agricultural areas (Walker 1986, 118), the work of the ALS concentrates on identifying and recording sites in that type of terrain. Afforestable Land Surveys are, exceptionally, funded by the tax payer and not developers. The programme is designed to select areas that are expected to have considerable archaeological remains. In some cases areas already under forestry, which are known to have had significant settlement (from cartographic, documentary sources, etc.), have been selected and adjacent unplanted areas surveyed. Survey areas are chosen before planting proposals are put in place and are identified through co-operation between the RCAHMS, Historic Scotland, the Forestry Commission and the Regional Archaeologist (Halliday and Ritchie *ibid.*).

Reconnaissance surveys are carried out initially and where the evidence on the ground is complex, a full-scale field survey is commissioned. Each survey is commissioned for an area of about 100km^2, and by 1992 an area of about 1,000km^2 had been covered (*ibid.*). Modern surveying techniques are used to survey large areas of land as efficiently as possible; for example, an area of 95 square kilometres in the Strath of Kildonan was surveyed in four to five months (RCAHMS 1993). Archaeological sites are recorded and identified to the Forestry Commission as areas which must be avoided by future forestry development. The ALS is concerned not only with ancient sites and monuments but equally with historic sites and landscapes, for example, post-medieval settlements, industrial processing areas and extraction sites.

In Scotland, as in Ireland, there has been a recent shift in planting trends from uplands to the better soils of the lowlands (Halliday and Ritchie 1992, 170). While the initial ALSs were carried out in upland and marginal areas, more attention is currently being paid to the threat to archaeology in the lowlands which is seen as a serious concern for the future (*ibid.*). For the moment, however, the ALS continues to target marginal upland areas.

WALES

As is the case in Scotland, the Welsh archaeological authorities interact closely with the forestry authorities.

While the scale of afforestation in Wales is not as extensive as in Scotland, CADW (Welsh Historic Monuments) has identified forestry as one of the main archaeological conservation concerns (Berry 1992, 155). The solution is seen as part of an integrated approach to archaeology and the environment, incorporating an overall countryside management strategy. Clwyd Archaeology Service, for example, has an on-going 'sites and landscape management programme' which aims to manage and promote archaeological monuments within their landscape settings (Berry 1995, 105). Archaeological monuments are regarded as being valuable not just as cultural features but as landscape features, wildlife habitats and as public amenities (*ibid.*, 111).

The general approach to archaeology in Wales is similar to that in Scotland, although the management structure differs somewhat from the rest of Britain. Regional Archaeological Trusts are responsible for sites and monuments within their areas. In addition, most County Councils have an Archaeological Services section which deals, initially, with all planting proposals submitted to Forest Enterprise (the Welsh Forestry Authority). The Archaeological Services assessment is based solely on the Sites and Monuments Record but it is then passed, with recommendations, to the Historic Environment Manager (HEM) of the region's Archaeological Trust. The Trust also receives relevant woodland management proposals such as tree felling licences. Liaising with Forest Enterprise, the HEM visits and develops a management 'prescription' for each site (Berry, pers. comm.). As is the case in Scotland, the visual framework of the monument and its associated environment is taken into consideration in the management programme. The Archaeological Trusts receive an annual payment from CADW to facilitate the necessary responses to new planting and to allow for site visits. Contact between the Trusts, HEM and Forest Enterprise is 'both frequent and successful' and archaeology is also included as a module in the Nation Diploma in Forestry (*ibid.*).

CHAPTER 6

Archaeology, Forestry and Land Use

INTRODUCTION

The relationship between archaeology, land use and the landscape is central to the protection and management of sites and monuments. Ireland has never had formal land use or landscape policies. Changes in rural activities and agricultural practices, however, have forced the issues into the limelight.

While the focus of this project is on archaeology and afforestation, it would be unrealistic to consider either subject in isolation from its overall relationship with agriculture. Within this context, one of the most significant considerations is the question of land use and the role of archaeology and forestry within land-use policies.

As well as the immediate practical and economic benefits derived by the farmer, land use affects the local community, the environment, the long term viability of the land, the ecology and the archaeology of the area. While these factors are inherently important, they are also important elements in one of the most significant growth industries in Western Europe — tourism and leisure activities. Ireland's strongest selling points, home and abroad, are still its countryside and its culture. Archaeology is an essential, although often subtle, element of both.

While awareness of archaeological issues has grown in recent years, archaeological sites have come under increasing threat from agricultural developments. Despite refined legal protection, land improvements and changes in land use will potentially impact on archaeology. The completion of Sites and Monuments Records has provided a reference database against which current destruction rates for known archaeological sites can be gauged. It is not possible, however, to estimate the numbers of unrecorded sites that have been lost in the past or that are currently being destroyed. Land use and changes in that use must, therefore, be considered for their impact on all archaeology and not just that which is recorded. Where traditional landscapes are being transformed, there must be additional protection for their inherent features. Without an all-embracing land-use strategy in place, this is not possible and conflicts are bound to arise, many of which impact adversely on archaeology.

TRADITIONAL LAND USE

In the absence of a national land-use policy, traditional farming practices have dictated the use to which land is put. In recent years, European grants have had a significant influence on agricultural practices.

Ireland has never had a formal land-use policy. Tradition, market prices of agricultural products and the ability of the area to sustain the most lucrative products have determined land use in the past. With the highest percentage of productive grassland in Europe, Irish agriculture has always relied heavily on dairy and beef farming. In 1985, 83% of agricultural land use was in those two sectors with only 6% under tillage (Dempsey 1995, 22). A variety of factors (the European Union, over-supplied markets, rural population decline, etc.) have influenced a shift in traditional farming. In recent years, government and European Union financial packages have encouraged new land-use patterns and changes in rural landscapes without any long-term policies having been in place. The introduction of grants for disadvantaged areas, for 'alternative' farming and for under-supplied markets, have had significant consequences, some of which have impacted on archaeology. Grant-driven or market-determined land use is rarely beneficial to the land and tends instead to favour the individual, often in an unsustainable manner (*ibid.*, 21).

The introduction of European Union grants for sheep, land reclamation and, most recently, forestry has altered traditional land use in the West of Ireland and the uplands in particular. There is, as yet, no guarantee that current grant levels will be sustained after the year 2000. Grant-aid can be suspended or restructured without warning. The suspension of grants for the important farm pollution prevention scheme, for example, or the current funding crisis for the REP scheme demonstrate the tenuous nature of agricultural grants. Emphasis is constantly changing (from uplands to lowlands, dairy to beef, crops to trees, etc.), depending on funds available from Europe.

Changing rural patterns
The current population decline in rural areas has had a number of negative effects on archaeology.

Much of the traditionally grazed moorlands and drier blanket bogs in Ireland have now been abandoned by the farming communities. The rural population has declined by an estimated 43,000 people since 1986 (D/AFF 1994a, 150) and a further 20,000 are expected to leave rural areas before the year 2001. The decline has already affected archaeology, particularly archaeological monuments which were maintained (actively or inactively) by traditional farming practices. A knowledge of the land and of archaeological sites goes hand-in-hand with most rural indigenous farmers, and local information has led to the discovery of many previously unrecorded sites and monuments. As the rural exodus continues, it takes with it a wealth of information and the folklore that is so often associated with sites.

Alternative farming
Forestry is considered as an 'alternative' form of agriculture, being promoted to entice farmers away from over-productive sectors.

Financial packages and directives from Brussels have had a significant impact on Irish farming and land use. Faced with low market prices and European food surpluses, those who have stayed in farming have been forced to consider alternative practices. The current trend is towards diversification into areas previously considered to be 'alternative', from deer and ostrich farming to agri-tourism and forestry. While some of these are entrepreneurial ventures, others are clearly grant-driven. With increasing pressure on Irish farmers to curtail production levels of milk, butter, cereals, etc., farmers look to Europe for grant-aided alternatives. Forestry is one of the most heavily promoted 'alternative' farm enterprises, with grants structured to favour full-time farmers.

Agricultural grants
Grants have been used to attempt to stem the continuing decline in rural depopulation. A balance must be achieved between economic returns and conservation of natural and archaeological heritage. Previous grant systems have caused long-term problems such as over-grazing.

There is general agreement in Europe that low-productivity farming and substantial financial assistance is preferable to rural depopulation. Therefore, the various payments and premia are considered to be an essential part of modern European agriculture. The imbalance between short-term economic gain and the possible long-term effects on the ecology, environment and archaeology has yet to be addressed. Grants intended to promote rural development may have the desired effects but may also have detrimental knock-on effects in other sectors. Dempsey (1995, 25) argues, for example, that the scenic and tourist values of traditionally grazed hills and marginal areas in the west of Ireland is too important to allow over-grazing, enclosure or the most recent introduction, afforestation. From a short-term, economic perspective, forestry is lucrative as an additional source of income to farmers. An ESRI report in 1993 on the impact of forestry on rural communities confirmed that employment and farm incomes can be significantly increased through forestry activities (Kearney 1995, 27). This is the only immediate benefit identified for small-scale, evergreen planting.

FORESTRY AS LAND USE
Promoted as an 'alternative' form of land use, forestry is developing into a lucrative aspect of Irish agriculture. There is, however, some debate over its distribution, management and long-term sustainability.

In the absence of a national land-use policy, individual policies have been, or are being, developed to govern individual issues involved in rural land use (e.g. tourism, agriculture, rural employment, depopulation and forestry). Ideally, these issues should be dealt with under an umbrella forum but the development of an all-embracing land-use policy would be so complex and would take so long that it 'could be out-of-date on the day it is launched' (Hickie 1994, 3). One of the difficulties with developing individual policies for land use is that they will often come into conflict with each other, with European grant structures and with issues which have not been fully considered within the policy. Forestry policy has largely been dictated by an annual planting target and a grant system designed to achieve that level of planting.

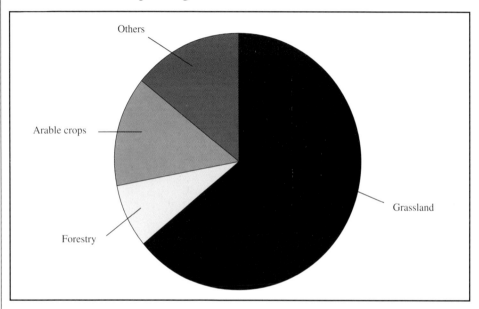

Fig. 19. *Land Use in Ireland. Rural land use is dominated by pasture (64%) with about 8% now under forestry.*

Roughly one million hectares of wet mineral lowlands are considered to be highly productive for forestry. In addition, there are many areas of Ireland where afforestation would have positive environmental benefits such as preventing erosion, providing diversification of habitats, etc., as well as blending in with or enhancing the landscape. There are other areas where afforestation would be detrimental to the archaeology, to the environment and to the landscape. The difficulty is that the controls in place at present do not identify these areas adequately so that unsuitable blanket bog is still being planted while potentially higher yield soils are being ignored. Dempsey (1995, 22-23) argues that a sensible land-use policy, from an agricultural point of view, would steer some of that land (about 20% of the country) away from the current dairying and dry stock farming and into forestry.

Forestry as multi-functional land use
The potential benefits for archaeology in forestry have yet to be considered. State public forests contain many archaeological and historical sites which can add diversity to the forests and enhance the overall forest environment.

Forestry has great potential to provide shelterbelts; amenity, conservation and recreation areas; for game production; and for tourism, but these options have been 'relatively ignored' until recently (Bulfin 1995, 39). Although multi-functional forestry is an option normally open only to larger land owners and State organisations, good management of forests means a woodland can serve many purposes. Le Forêt de Soignes, just outside Brussels, for example, has over a million visitors per year while being 'one of the most productive and beautiful beech forests in Europe'

(Hummel 1983, 30). The fact that such ambitions are long-term proposals reinforces the need to consider forestry as a sustainable form of land use. The agri-tourism and the leisure industries are growing and there will undoubtedly be a role for smaller developments. There is an increasingly significant role for forestry in providing outdoor recreational facilities to meet the growing public demand in Ireland (e.g. Gardiner 1991, 348; McCormack and O'Leary 1993). Given the simultaneous growth of interest in heritage issues, it follows that there is a tremendous opportunity to combine all interests, commercial, recreational, educational and archaeological.

ENVIRONMENTAL ISSUES

Environmental concerns are of primary importance in land-use policies. Natural and heritage conservation share many common concerns. Closer contact between environmental and archaeological sectors would provide a forum for management of conservation issues. The Danish 'historic' approach to land-use policies demonstrates how a variety of seemingly conflicting factors can be effectively integrated. Similarly, Historic Scotland and Scottish Natural Heritage promote co-operation and co-ordination of their respective concerns.

Trees are a natural part of a landscape and can therefore be incorporated into land use as an appropriate and beneficial element. To achieve a balance, however, associated issues such as nature conservation, environmental protection, agriculture, tourism and archaeology have to be considered in an overall plan. Well thought-out forest policies, practices and management are essential to a sustainable forest industry. While the Forest Service and some forest companies have policies in place which promote such issues, the wide-ranging objections to afforestation suggest that such policies are not adequate.

Public and political awareness of the need to protect important natural habitats is probably at an all-time high. There are now strict guidelines within the European Union on the conservation and protection of important environments and there is a legitimate case to be made for regarding nature conservation as a form of land use in itself with inherent economic and social benefits (e.g. Hickie 1990, 24). Furthermore, if it is accepted that our cultural heritage is a primary tourist attraction, combining the two forms creates a strong case for direct input into the issue of land use in Ireland. It is generally acknowledged abroad that a close association exists between natural and heritage conservation. Bog/peatland, for example, is regarded as a precious source of both wildlife and archaeological remains and is 'non-renewable' (Yarnell 1993, 29). While archaeology, ecology and the environment are distinct disciplines, they share many issues and common concerns. Archaeology can benefit from environmental controls such as protection of bogland or designation of Natural Heritage Areas.

The Danish approach to land use, heritage and nature conservation is particularly interesting and progressive. Protection of archaeology is the responsibility of the National Forest and Nature Agency (Kristiansen 1988; see also Anon b 1995). While conflicts of interest might be expected to pose insurmountable problems, the agency appears to avoid them by taking an 'historic view' of nature as the basis of policy formulation (Kristiansen 1992). Land is not classified solely on its productive capability but is also considered in terms of its historic significance. The forces which developed the landscape (human activity in the past, natural generation and change, etc.) are given equal respect in deciding appropriate land use and conservation activities.

Historic Scotland and Scottish Natural Heritage have recently issued a statement of intent along these lines. Conservation of natural and heritage features in Scotland, as far as is possible, are given equal importance. Therefore lichens on an ancient bridge, for example, are treated as being of equal significance to the bridge itself. Any repair work done on the bridge must respect the habitat of the lichens.

TOURISM
Tourism is a major growth industry in Ireland. New aspects are being developed, such as farm and rural-based activity holidays.

As a growth industry (worth an estimated £900 million per year) tourism in Ireland depends largely on the natural and cultural heritage. The tourism industry has 'very much focused on special interest visitors, and on developing the product potential of historical and archaeological sites and landscapes' (Cooney 1991, 70). This is reflected in the number of interpretative centres and sites with visitor facilities as well as in the overall increasing awareness of heritage issues in rural areas. Power (1993, 139) notes the increase in local historical and archaeological groups over the past decade, while Cooney (1993, 19) cites Bórd Fáilte figures of 1.3 million overseas tourists having visited archaeological and historical sites in the 1990/91 season. There is a general realisation that archaeology can be exploited in a positive manner but it must be controlled and managed to ensure the long-term survival of the sites and monuments.

The current buzz word 'agri-tourism' is high on the list of potential growth areas within the sector. In March 1995, the government announced a major agri-tourism initiative under the European Union's Operational Programme for Agriculture, Rural Development and Forestry (D/AFF 1994a). The main aim of the grant-aided scheme is to promote activity and leisure in rural Ireland and to entice a more interactive form of holiday in the 'countryside'. Archaeology and forestry are significant factors in the development of rural tourism and there are mutual benefits to be derived from interactive management schemes.

PREHISTORIC LAND USE
There is not necessarily a correlation between present and prehistoric land use. It is not possible, therefore, to conclude that marginal agricultural land has always been of limited value or thinly settled.

When discussing land use there is often a tendency to correlate present day use with prehistoric use. Factors which affect farming activities, such as climate, soil type, drainage and the activities of people are not static elements and have changed through time. Marginal and bogland areas, for example, were not always marginal or bog lands. Beneath blanket bog at Carrownaglogh, Co. Mayo, for example, the discovery of cultivation ridges suggests that such upland areas may have been more fertile in the past (O'Connell 1991, 67). In addition, if the presence of wedge tombs is taken as an indicator of nearby prehistoric activity (see, for example, Grogan 1991), the concentration of tombs in upland areas of the West and South suggests that there may have been substantial upland settlement, at least periodically, in the past.

Therefore areas that are of low agricultural value to-day may well have been relatively productive and farmed in the past. Defining prehistoric landscapes and economies, however, is one of the most complex aspects of archaeological study. Information takes many forms including animal and plant remains from excavations, pollen analysis of surrounding soils, distribution of monuments and artefacts and systematic field surveying of whole areas. To gain an understanding of prehistory, sites must be examined within the broad context of their contemporary cultures, economies, climate and environments. Sites which are preserved and protected as isolated buffered zones will yield only limited information.

Lowlands
Forestry has moved into lowland areas in recent years because of a restructuring in grants for planting. While these areas are relatively well-covered by Ordnance Survey maps, they are largely unexplored by modern

The lowlands present different problems and require different solutions for identifying and protecting archaeology. Good quality low-lying land was extensively settled throughout the country but the traces of that settlement are not always obvious. Many archaeological sites, such as house foundations, are normally only identified through intensive surveying techniques. Lowland settlement sites also used to be put into the broader context of

scientific detection methods and aerial photography.

their surrounding environment of fields, forest, water. Early timber houses and associated field boundaries of wood or earthen banks have, however, long since decayed into subsoil traces, overlaid by later patterns of settlement. Thousands of years of intensive settlement radically alter drainage, boundaries and land use. It is, however, possible to detect archaeological sites under pasture or under crops using a range of surveying techniques (see Chapter 1).

Uplands and marginal lands
Upland and marginal areas of Ireland were targeted for afforestation throughout the 60s, 70s and 80s. Although there is a drive away from marginal soils, the distribution of forestry in Ireland will probably always remain centred on these areas. Areas in which agriculture has been relatively restricted are important refuges for archaeological sites and monuments.

The definition of 'upland' areas will vary depending on regional geography. If a standard height of 800ft is used to define uplands, only about 5% of Ireland is included. In most of Ireland, however, terrain over about 400ft is considered to be high or upland and the soils in these area are generally of poor quality. Marginal zones, likewise, depend on regional variations and the ability of the land to sustain agriculture. In strictly agricultural terms over 50% of Ireland is now considered marginal or less favoured 'due to wetness, shallow soils, steep slopes, organic soils, rockiness or adverse climate' (Dunstan 1985, 104). Approximately 21% of this is in the high yield category for forestry, mainly wet mineral lowland soils (*ibid.*). It is estimated that there are over 800,000 hectares of marginal farm land in Ireland (Hickie 1990, 16).

Early State planting was concentrated in the south-east of the country but as planting techniques improved and equipment was developed, the boglands and uplands of Munster and Connaught were heavily planted. Afforestation gradually moved into marginal agricultural land and more recently into the wet mineral lowland soils (Dunstan 1985, 104).

The structure of archaeological sites found in the upland and marginal areas will often differ from those in the lowlands. Stone monuments, for example, are more common in marginal areas while the lowlands have a predominance of earthen structures. The thinner soils of the uplands would not have allowed construction of earthworks whereas the predominance of stone lent itself to building in stone. Survival of sites and monuments in the two areas will also differ. Marginal and upland areas have generally suffered less from development, and therefore archaeology which exists there will often survive in more complete form. The dichotomy between historical land use in uplands and lowlands has led to a situation where many lowland sites have been destroyed through repeated ploughing while those in the uplands have been left to a greater extent intact. This has created, to a varying extent, an artificial monument distribution.

In more recent years, the introduction of sheep headage payments resulted in extensive overgrazing of upland and marginal areas, and undoubtedly has caused much damage and destruction of archaeological sites. The expansion of state forestry in the 1950s, 1960s and 1970s has probably had an even more drastic impact on upland archaeology. The most obvious damage has been to stone structures — the extent of the damage caused to less visible sites cannot be estimated. An IAPA report on the impact of forestry on archaeology suggested that the highest rates of site-destruction occurred in the very marginal regions 'which are least well documented by the OS maps' (Foley *et al.* 1991, 2).

Bogland and peatland
Bogland is internationally one of the most important habitats requiring protection. It is also an important repository of archaeological objects and information. It is estimated that less than 10% of the original bog cover of Ireland remains. While some is now protected by various nature and environmental directives, there is still widespread exploitation of blanket and raised boglands. Coillte now has a policy of not acquiring any further intact bogland, but the company still relies heavily on planting in marginal areas of degraded bogland.

Ireland has the second highest proportion of peatland in Europe and the few remaining intact raised bogs are internationally recognised as areas of world renown and importance. Exploitation and destruction of bogland on a large scale began this century with commercial peat cutting, reclamation, over-grazing and afforestation. It is estimated that approximately 90% of the original 800,000 hectares (almost 2 million acres) of blanket bogland has been severely destroyed or degraded this century. Less than 10% of the original bog cover is left and that figure is continuing to decline through peat extraction, grazing and more recently afforestation. Many areas have now been designated as Areas of Scientific Interest or proposed Natural Heritage Areas and are therefore protected from interference, but the vast majority of blanket bogland remains under threat, particularly from afforestation. Similarly, European Union Directives on the Conservation of Wild Birds and on Natural Habitats go some way towards protecting selected areas of blanket bog.

In 1982 the Irish Peatland Conservation Council (IPCC) was formed to lobby at national and international levels for the conservation of raised bogs. In 1986 the International Mire Conservation Group identified the Irish blanket bogs as being 'unique and of global importance' (Irish Peatland Conservation Council 1989). Europe had previously acknowledged the significance of boglands in its Resolution on the Protection of Irish Bogs (European Parliament 1983). In 1991 an agreement between the European Commission, the OPW and Bórd na Móna was reached to conserve the few remaining intact raised bogs and to reinstate some of the less damaged bogs. Some of the pressure for bog preservation originates in the Netherlands, where over a quarter of a million pounds is spent annually in an attempt to reinstate the tiny proportion of bogland remaining.

Boglands occur in three forms in Ireland: blanket bogs, raised bogs and fenlands. All three types have been exploited in different ways, blanket bogs and moorlands, in particular, having been targeted for afforestation. Blanket bogland tends to be shallower than raised bog and covers large areas of mountain and flatland alike. It forms in regions where the annual rainfall is relatively high and can range in depth from about 2m to 8m. Much of the blanket bogland in the West of Ireland probably began to spread during the Bronze Age when the climate became wetter and cooler than before (O'Connell 1991, 66). Climatic fluctuations alone, however, were not responsible for the formation. The impact of deforestation and (relatively) intensive farming, which degraded the soil and vegetation, had apparently a significant influence on its formation (*ibid.*).

The Irish Government in 1989 imposed a target area for conservation of blanket peatland of 40,000 hectares which is estimated as 5.2% of the original area of blanket peatland (Farrell and Kelly-Quinn 1991, 355). In addition, Coillte has indicated that it no longer intends acquiring blanket peatland and is disposing of much that is currently in its ownership (McLoughlin, pers. comm.). The decision was taken largely on economic grounds — while the hardier spruce species grow well on peatland their yield is consistently lower than on better mineral soils. Despite this, however, Coillte is still planting on the Western seaboard and much of this afforestation is of peatland, which is considered to be degraded in environmental terms but which may still be rich archaeological repositories. Similarly, Bord na Móna, the State peat company, intends to convert some of its exhausted bogland, much of it raised bog to forestry and has identified *c.* 50,000 hectares of cutaway bogland as being suitable for afforestation (D/AFF 1996, 19, 3.5). The Strategic Plan for the Development of the Forestry Sector in Ireland (D/AFF 1996) recommends encouraging planting on this land but cautions that pilot studies will be required.

Archaeology in bogland
While the environmental significance of bogland is widely acknowledged, their importance to archaeology is not always realised. The work of the Irish Archaeological Wetland Unit has demonstrated the archaeological potential of degraded and cut-over raised bogs.

While the significance of boglands as floral and faunal habitats is widely recognised, their importance for archaeology is less evident. Extensive studies at Behy/Glenulra (Caulfield 1983) make it clear that early farmers settled upland regions, but that peat growth began relatively soon after, covering over and effectively fossilising a very early agricultural landscape of stone-walled fields. There is no doubt that many such archaeological landscapes lie under the blanket bog elsewhere, of critical importance to prehistoric studies. Within a bog certain conditions exist which allow for excellent preservation of organic material. The waterlogged nature of bogland restricts microbial activity which would normally destroy organic remains.

The Irish Archaeological Wetland Unit (IAWU) was established by the OPW in 1990 as a response to the massive exploitation of the midland's raised bogs. Raised bogs, which can be over 10m deep, often originated as lakes, attractive to early hunter gatherers whose slight settlements can be preserved by the growth of peat. Later bog users left behind a wide range of artefacts (wooden vessels, metalwork, boats, human bodies, clothing, etc.) and features (trackways, settlement camps, etc.). To date, over eleven hundred timber trackways, dating mostly to the Bronze Age, have been recorded by the IAWU. One of the most impressive toghers identified is that at Corlea, Co. Longford, which was constructed of huge oak planks and ran for almost two kilometres through the raised bog. There are hundreds of less extensive 'toghers' throughout Ireland which would not have been preserved without the anaerobic conditions of the boglands. The shallower blanket bogs similarly mask and preserve organic material as well as stone and metal artefacts and structures. Blanket bogs are not, however, included in the brief of the Wetlands Unit and their exploitation has been widespread and uncontrolled.

It is no co-incidence that many of the outstanding areas of natural beauty are also rich in archaeology. What adds to their beauty is their relatively untouched nature, unaffected by modern development, agriculture and housing. The relative absence of modern development increases their potential as areas of extensive archaeological preservation; landscapes from the past preserved by bog and moor. Archaeological landscapes, however, are not only preserved in bog and moorland settings. The prehistoric complexes at Lough Gur (eg. Ó Ríordáin 1954; Cleary 1993) or Knockroe (Condit and O'Sullivan 1995) in County Limerick, demonstrate the use of a range of locations, from hill-tops to lake-sides, to low-lying pasture land. Throughout the country, archaeology forms part of the landscape, from the old field systems of the West to the dominant structures of Dun Aonghusa or Newgrange. Archaeology is not just a visible aspect of the landscape, but an integral part of what formed the landscape itself. Archaeology must, therefore, be regarded as an essential factor in any formulation of an overall land-use strategy for Ireland. It is, however, only in recent years that the concept of managing archaeology as a 'major element in the landscape' has been recognised (see, for examples, Macinnes 1993, 243; Grogan *et al.* 1995). Consequently, the relationship between archaeology and current land uses has yet to be clearly defined.

CHAPTER 7

Conclusions and Recommendations

INTRODUCTION

The following conclusions and recommendations are presented as points for further discussion and, in some cases, for further research. While some of the recommendations would require substantial financial input and therefore will merit further research and investigation, some are procedural and could be implemented by the Forest Service, foresters and landowners at minimal costs.

PROTECTION OF ARCHAEOLOGICAL MONUMENTS

Comprehensive legal protection exists for National Monuments and for archaeological sites that are entered in the Register of Historic Monuments and/or the Record of Monuments and Places. In addition to the National Monuments Acts (1930-1994), the Irish Government has ratified the European Convention on the Protection of the Archaeological Heritage (The Valletta Convention). Amongst other agreements, the Government must now ensure the involvement of archaeologists in the planning and development processes. The recent changes in local authority planning regulations should improve the degree of contact between archaeologists and planners at local level — it remains to be seen how effective the system will be.

The potential impact of afforestation on archaeological sites
Sufficient evidence exists to state that afforestation can have a potentially detrimental effect on archaeological sites and monuments. The extent of that damage cannot be estimated without field-based assessment. An assessment of sites that are known to exist in forestry would assist in the formulation of management policies.

The potential threat to archaeological sites from afforestation and forestry has been acknowledged abroad and in Ireland. The IAPA report on damage to archaeological sites and the assessment of the archaeological inventories for West and Mid Cork (see Appendix 2) provide some evidence of the impact of afforestation. The fieldwork carried out in the course of this research was intended only to attain a general level of understanding of the processes involved in afforestation in Ireland. It was not designed to identify actual instances of damage to, or destruction of, archaeological sites. A more detailed, field-based assessment, perhaps of a number of sample areas, would be required to estimate the extent of the damage caused by afforestation. Nonetheless, during the research, four cases of damage to Recorded Monuments were reported, and two unrecorded archaeological sites were identified as being at risk from surrounding forestry. Combined, these examples indicate the need for positive action to mitigate the damage already caused, and to prevent further destruction of archaeological sites and monuments.

The additional impact of forestry on archaeological landscapes is also a significant factor in the planning and management of forestry. Ireland is experiencing an unprecedented level of planting that will shape many parts of the countryside for decades to come. While considerable effort is being made to plan forestry in a visually sensitive manner, the archaeological landscape has not been taken into consideration and consequently sites and monuments have been isolated from their surroundings. Identifying, protecting and managing archaeological sites can only be addressed by comprehensive and co-operative means and through sustainable planning and management.

89

> • *Assessment of a sample of archaeological sites known to exist in forestry would clarify the nature and extent of damage caused to archaeological sites by afforestation. It would also provide information on which to base management policy and procedures to reduce the potential impact of afforestation on the archaeological heritage.*

Recorded Monuments
The forestry sector must receive continuously updated information on Recorded Monuments and Places. The preliminary status of the register, however, must be emphasised.

All grant-aided planting applications are checked by the Forest Service inspectors against the Record of Monuments and Places. The role of the Record is therefore central to the protection of known archaeology in forestry and in areas to be afforested. The tendency to regard the record as a definitive list of the archaeology in an area, however, must be discouraged. It is intended to serve only as a preliminary inventory of known sites.

It is also essential that the information is updated regularly and presented to the Forest Service, to the self-regulating companies, and to local agricultural organisations such as Teagasc, Forbairt, REPS officers, etc.

> • *Over-reliance on the Record of Monuments and Places must be avoided and its preliminary status must be emphasised. The lists must be continuously updated and distributed to the Forest Service, the larger forestry companies, and those with control over agricultural/forestry activities in the regions.*

Unrecorded archaeological sites
Emphasis must be placed on identifying unrecorded sites and low-visibility archaeology.

While procedures can be implemented to protect known sites, the identification of buried, or partially buried sites is fraught with practical difficulties. Sub-soil archaeology forms an essential core of archaeological information and for some periods is the only surviving evidence. This issue reinforces the need for professional assessment by archaeologists and for monitoring of areas to be planted. The revised Forest Service guidelines on forestry and archaeology must emphasise the importance of recognising and protecting sites that exist below ground level. Archaeology must also be introduced as a significant module in forestry training and educational courses on forest establishment and management.

> • *Identifying and protecting unrecorded archaeological sites requires input from professional archaeologists in forestry training and education courses. It also requires a more direct form of contact and consultation between archaeologists and foresters during the planting process.*

Inventory of sites in forestry
There is an urgent need for an inventory of sites in existing forestry.

In order to respond to the threat from afforestation, it is necessary to identify those sites that already exist in forestry. In some cases, it is possible to extract such information from other sources; The Cork Archaeological Inventories (Power 1992; 1994; 1997), for example, record the land-use associated with the individual sites at the time of visiting. It is, therefore, possible to identify sites known to exist in forestry in Co. Cork (see Appendix 2). Most archaeological inventories, however, do not include information on land use.

> • *In future the Archaeological Inventories should record and publish the land-use associated with sites.*

An alternative approach would be possible with the co-operation of the Forestry Service. The Forest Service is currently compiling an updated inventory of forestry in Ireland. Given that SMR information is already available in GIS format, forest distribution could be incorporated into the system to allow the existence and distribution of sites in forestry to be assessed and monitored. This would allow for priority sites to be visited in order to assess their condition and would facilitate the formulation of management policies and strategies.

- *An inventory of archaeological sites in existing forestry would allow a more complete assessment of the situation and would facilitate management policies and plans for their future.*

Pre-Afforestation field surveying
Unrecorded sites will be damaged or destroyed once an area is planted. Thorough field-based assessment, in conjunction with other forms of analysis, and monitoring during the planting preparation would facilitate protection and management of sites.

While recorded sites face a variety of threats throughout the forest cycle, unrecorded sites are probably most at risk from afforestation and require action in the form of a strategy for identification and protection pre-afforestation. The introduction of pre-planting field surveys is one possible response, but the type of survey would have to be tailored to the individual application for planting. In some cases, appropriate surveying would require extensive fieldwork using a range of detection equipment and techniques. In other cases, monitoring of the actual planting process might be more productive.

In either case, financing such survey work will be the most contentious issue. Is it reasonable to expect large forestry companies to pay for surveying pre-afforestation? Is it reasonable to demand the same requirements of an individual farmer? The forestry industry is heavily financed by the European Union and Irish Government. Substantial grants are available for most private planting (with the exception of Christmas trees). If the situation is reversed and the impact of archaeology on afforestation is considered, the case is, perhaps, clearer. In lieu of a considerable financial grant, a forestry developer is required only to ensure that the initial planting and associated activities do not damage a previously recorded archaeological site. Archaeological consultation is carried out between the Forest Service and the National Monuments and Historic Properties Service (NMHPS), and therefore no costs are incurred by the landowner.

Although it is an informal procedure, the unplanted area around a monument is normally included in the calculation of the grant — in effect, the landowner is compensated for not planting around the sensitive zone. Given that the level of funding for private planting is between 80-100% of the total costs, a portion of that might be allocated for archaeological assessment pre-planting. In many cases, the cost of archaeological assessment would comprise a fee and expenses for a professional archaeologist for a single day. There are no set rates for archaeological services, but a basic assessment of an area would not be costly. Given that the most basic afforestation grant (that for unenclosed land) is £975 per hectare, not including the maintenance grant, the cost of archaeological assessment in many cases would not be excessive. Where the proposed planting involves a large area of archaeological potential, the financial costs of archaeological impact assessment will obviously be greater; in exceptional cases, where extensive investigation is required, the costs (and the archaeological implications) might be prohibitive.

Funding for forestry research and development is provided under the European Union Operational Programme for Forestry. Research on the impact of forestry on the environment is financed under that scheme. The contrast between funding of the forestry industry and the lack of funding for the practical protection of archaeology is striking. Cooney (1993, 19) speculates on how the balance between forestry and archaeology would be redressed if 'even half of the level of grant aid afforded to forest planting...was given to the protection, preservation and presentation of suitable archaeological sites, complexes and landscapes in rural areas of Ireland'. Realistically such a balance is not expected, but the industry must be brought into line with developments in other areas where the developer contributes to necessary archaeological conditions. Large-scale afforestation programmes, carried out by commercial companies, must involve archaeological consultation and pre-development assessment. Similarly, where a planting programme is likely to adversely impact on archaeology, the developer must demonstrate that adequate protective measures are in place to avoid damage to recorded and unrecorded sites.

- *The initial risks to archaeological sites could be reduced through consultation with archaeologists and through field-based assessment pre-afforestation. The costs of archaeological assessment must be borne by the developer, but financial assistance from the forestry programme could reasonably be expected for pre-planting inspection of planting proposals.*

- *To ensure continued protection for archaeological sites in forests, landowners must be actively encouraged to maintain sites free of overgrowth and to ensure protection against accidental damage from machinery, wind-throw, etc. Forest managers should not be financially penalised through the loss of income for protecting archaeological sites. Compensation for such management could be provided by formally including the unplanted 'buffer zone' in the calculation of the forest grant.*

Environmental Impact Assessments
Procedures and methodologies for pre-afforestation archaeological assessment must be standardised and monitored.

At present, the only form of pre-afforestation archaeological surveying is through the EIA process. While the vast majority of planting is still under 30 hectares and therefore will not be brought into the assessment process, new regulations are now in place to incorporate contiguous planting into the EIA system, and to provide local authorities with greater control over planting in their areas. Previous research, however, suggests that the standard of archaeological impact assessments is not always adequate. This needs to be re-evaluated and a code of practice and/or guidelines introduced for carrying out the surveys. The limitations of the EIA process, particularly with respect to low-visibility archaeology, must be acknowledged within the afforestation process.

- *Reassessment of the standards of archaeological impact assessment, and the introduction of a code of practice for pre-development surveying, are required.*

Archaeological survey unit for forestry
A pre-afforestation field unit would contribute significantly to the identification and protection of sites.

Establishing a survey unit along the lines of the Scottish Afforestable Land Survey would be a costly and time-consuming exercise. Unquestionably, given the positive results from the various Scottish surveys, it would be a worthy project. In the context of current planting trends, however, it should, perhaps, be considered as an independent objective rather than as an immediate and appropriate response to the expansion of forestry. Planting is now dominated by the private sector, over 80% of which is farm-based. A central archaeological survey unit could not cope with the number of individual applications for planting. The response to these must be based on local or regional assessment.

A dual-purpose unit, however, could serve to co-ordinate contract archaeologists working with forestry developments, and to carry out selective pre-afforestation surveys. Detailed survey for larger commercial developments could be carried out by such a unit. In addition, selective areas considered as being of high potential for archaeological sites could also be identified by the unit so that afforestation could be discouraged within them. The pilot Indicative Forestry Scheme took cognisance of recorded archaeological sites and has afforded them additional protection from afforestation. There is a need, however, for further archaeological investigation of the areas identified as suitable for afforestation.

- *The establishment of an archaeological unit, specifically intended to investigate areas pre-afforestation, would not be capable of responding to current forestry trends. It would, however, be useful for carrying out large-scale pre-afforestation surveys, and for co-ordinating individual assessments of proposed planting areas. In co-operation with the Forest Service, such a unit could be deployed to investigate areas targeted for afforestation by Indicative Forestry Schemes.*

Monitoring of the planting process
To identify unrecorded sites, monitoring of planting procedures is necessary.

Regardless of whether or not a pre-planting survey is carried out, monitoring of the planting preparation must be considered. It is only after ploughing or excavation of drainage systems that a realistic assessment of 'low-visibility' archaeology can take place. While by their nature both processes will cause damage to archaeological sites, further damage and destruction will be prevented by investigation during and after the operations.

This will become increasingly necessary as planting moves into the better-quality land where traces of prehistoric settlement would be expected. Planting near existing monuments, in areas already known to be rich in prehistoric remains, or in prime locations for prehistoric settlement (rivers, lakes, cut-over bogs, etc.) should be monitored by an experienced field archaeologist. The process of introducing forestry to pasture land in particular, may provide archaeology with the first opportunity to assess what lies below the ground.

- *Monitoring of the planting process, by an experienced archaeologist, would provide an opportunity to identify unrecorded sites and allow appropriate action to be taken.*

The Strategic Plan for the Development of the Forestry Sector in Ireland has established the policy for forestry to the year 2030. It envisages a sustained programme of planting an average of 20,000 hectares (49,500 acres) per annum, with continued emphasis on private, farm-based planting. While current funding for the programme is secure to the end of the century, previous experiences demonstrate the uncertain nature of policies formulated on the basis of grant structures.

The majority of forestry activities at present are grant-aided and therefore various controls are in place. Given the extensive nature of the programme, the controls must now be re-assessed and reinforced to ensure compliance. In the case of non grant-aided planting, however, there are no additional regulations to prevent damage to archaeological sites and monuments. A system of assessment of such activities is required.

- *The current forestry policy in relation to archaeological sites and monuments must be enforced in practice through monitoring and field-based inspection of sites. Regulations regarding archaeology and afforestation need to be introduced to include all planting and not just that which is grant-aided.*

Compliance with the Forest Service guidelines on forestry and archaeology.

Coillte Teoranta has received much criticism in recent years for its planting programme. One of the negative effects of this has been to draw attention away from the activities of other forestry companies and private planters. While Coillte has a company policy on the protection of archaeology and has a number of Environmental Officers in place, most private forestry companies rely solely on the guidelines and procedures requested by the Forest Service. Regardless of the size of the operation, all grant-assisted planting must abide by Forest Service guidelines. To achieve compliance in practice, ground-level contact between professional archaeologists and the forestry sector will have to be formally established. Local authorities must insist that planting in designated sensitive areas is avoided, curtailed, or adequately controlled to avoid damaging archaeological sites. Given the large number of archaeological sites that must exist on Coillte property, the company must be encouraged to employ a professional and experienced field archaeologist to assess the condition of those sites and to develop a management strategy for ensuring their continued protection.

- *The National Monuments Acts, the Forest Service guidelines on archaeology and local authority planning regulations must be complied with by all forestry companies, contractors and farmers. In order to achieve compliance in practice, comprehensive ground-level contact between the archaeological authorities and the forestry sector will have to be formally established.*

- *Coillte must be encouraged to employ at least one professional archaeologist to oversee compliance with the Forest Service guidelines, and to assess the condition of sites which already exist within its forestry.*

The Forest Service enforces the guidelines on archaeology to the extent that its officers can practically manage. Forest Service Inspectors carry out spot-checks on a regular basis. The increased interest from the private sector, however, has placed the service under considerable pressure and the degree to which random checks can be carried out varies from one county to the next. Limited field-work carried out in the compilation of this research indicated that Forest Service guidelines are not always adhered to, particularly as the forestry matures. To fully assess the extent to which the guidelines are enforced in practice, a more extensive survey of monuments in forestry would be required, and would initially require the compilation of an inventory of sites in forestry. It would, ultimately, be a valuable tool for organising future management schemes.

- *The degree of compliance with the Forest Service Guidelines on Archaeology needs to be determined through field-based assessment of existing sites in forestry. If it is found to be generally low, a more rigorous method of enforcement will have to be introduced.*

Raising awareness of archaeological sites

There is an onus on those involved in planting operations to ensure that recorded archaeological sites are not interfered with by forestry developments. There is, however, a practical need to inform foresters of the potential dangers which may face sites. To identify previously unrecorded sites and to raise the general awareness of archaeology before planting takes place, a question regarding the presence of archaeological sites in the proposed area could be included on the planting grant application form.

> • *A question regarding the presence of archaeological sites in an area to be planted would serve a dual purpose — to identify previously unrecorded sites and to raise awareness of the need to protect archaeological sites from developments such as forestry.*

Non-grant-aided planting

While the Forest Service can enforce some degree of protection for archaeological sites in grant-aided plantations, a system for monitoring non-grant-aided planting is required.

> • *Non-grant-aided planting requires assessment to ensure that it does not interfere with archaeological sites and monuments.*

Management of archaeology in forestry
Responsibility for the protection and management of archaeological sites in forestry must be designated. Issues such as access to and maintenance of sites within forestry have to be addressed.

Managing archaeology within the landscape does not have to be a rigid and conservative endeavour. The landscape has and always will be in a state of fluctuation and change, sometimes gradual and sometimes more immediate and drastic. Consequently, the response to change must be equally varied and flexible. A forested environment may be an ideal and appropriate setting for many archaeological monuments provided they are afforded the required management.

Responsibility for site management, however, must be addressed. The unplanted 'buffer zone' around a site will not remain free of vegetation throughout the life cycle of the forestry. Where an area has been traditionally maintained free of vegetation by grazing, for example, the overgrowth is likely to cause damage to the site and where natural regeneration of forestry threatens a particularly sensitive site, it must be controlled. Access to sites for maintenance and/or amenity purposes is necessary. The forestry sector does not assume responsibility for management of archaeological sites and the NMHPS does not have the structure or the resources to do so. As already suggested, an incentive to maintaining sites and ensuring their protection could be introduced by including the area left unplanted in the grant payments. Ultimately, however, the legal responsibility to avoid damage to recorded sites rests with the landowner.

> • *Management and maintenance of archaeological sites in forestry must be introduced if their long-term survival is to be ensured. Where sites are particularly fragile and/or under threat, specific management procedures must be enforced.*

Demarcation of sites in forestry

There is an additional and realistic danger that sites which are overgrown and obscured by vegetation will not be identified as protected areas when thinning or harvesting occurs. The current guideline requiring an 'appropriate buffer zone' (Forest Service b) to be left unplanted around a site is probably adequate for many sites providing it is maintained throughout the forest cycle. Defining the extremities of many sites, however, will require consultation with the archaeological authorities. The full extent of many earthworks, for example, will not always be obvious to the untrained eye and the possibility of associated low-visibility archaeology also needs to be considered. The introduction of standardised, easily recognisable marking stakes is required to avoid damage at all stages in the forest cycle, particularly to the more fragile or sensitive sites. Planting of broadleaf trees at a safe distance around an archaeological site in a coniferous plantation would serve as an attractive alternative, particularly in forestry intended for recreational use.

> • *Unambiguous marking of the protected buffer zone must be introduced and maintained throughout the life cycle of the forest plantation to ensure protection of archaeological sites, particularly during felling operations.*

Inter-site visibility

While the Forest Service has guidelines on forestry and its impact on the landscape, it does not consider the visual impact of forestry on archaeological monuments. Where groups of associated monuments occur, the sites should not be isolated from each other by having trees planted completely around them. Associated groups should, where at all possible, be maintained as interconnected sites by leaving larger areas of land unplanted. With adequate planning pre-afforestation, groups of associated monuments could be incorporated into clearings within the plantation. The contextual integrity of other sites must also be considered, for example, sites deliberately situated with a dominant aspect over their surrounds.

> • *Inter-site visibility and the context of an archaeological site or group of sites within the landscape must be considered as part of the normal forest planning.*

LAND-USE AND LANDSCAPE POLICIES
An integrated approach to archaeology and associated disciplines is required.

There are no all-embracing policies on land-use and landscape management in Ireland. In the absence of a national land-use policy, however, conflicts between forestry, 'traditional' agricultural practices, landscape and heritage issues will continue to arise. To deal with such conflicts, there must be a comprehensive policy on management of archaeology (in general and in particular situations such as in forestry). Closer contact and co-operation with farming organisations, co-operatives, forestry companies, etc. is also necessary to ensure practical protection and management of archaeology.

> • *A policy of management for archaeological sites in forestry is required to facilitate participation in the development of land-use and landscape policies.*

Multi-functional forestry
Archaeological sites are a positive feature within forestry.

Forestry has tremendous potential as a multi-functional form of land use which incorporates a variety of considerations within the forest environment. This is already recognised to a limited extent by Coillte Teoranta who maintain some of the State's forests as open, recreational facilities. Forests can be managed as productive commercial crops as well as serving as recreational features of the landscape. Within such forests, archaeology can play a significant role, enhancing the forest environment and contributing to the educational aspects of the reserves. Sites within such forests, however, need to be managed to ensure that they are not damaged by increased public access.

> • *Archaeology can be considered as an asset within forestry, particularly that which is intended for amenity, recreation and tourism. There must, however, be more active involvement from professional archaeologists to ensure that promotion of sites is carried out in an appropriate manner.*

PRACTICAL IMPLICATIONS

The above suggestions require, to varying degrees, a readjustment of aspects of forestry and archaeological practices. Fundamentally, they demand closer contact and co-operation between the two sectors and their associated organisations. The following suggestions are offered as possible

because of extensive network of drainage trenches (D *c.* 0.5-1.5m × W *c.* 1-1.5m) throughout field. Access will be extremely difficult, if not impossible, once trees mature.

The site is prepared for planting, ie., small mounds of soil have been placed over and around it but are not planted. A buffer zone of roughly 10m around the site is left unplanted but a drainage trench runs north-east/south-west approximately two metres to west of site. A low wooden stake to east marks site but is not obvious.

Site consists of roughly ovoid and irregular mound with track-like damage through it (not recent). No obvious original opening. Irregular central depression. Mound measures *c.* 9m N-S; *c.* 10m E-W; H *c.* 0.85m (ext) and H *c.* 0.75m (int). Forestry machinery damage is evident on north-western side of site where it exposed a section (*c.* 3.5m x 1.5m) through a dense mound of red, shattered and angular stones with some burnt organic material.

4. KNOCKNAKILLA (2)

OS 6" Map:	*CO 048*
Site Type:	*Circular Enclosure*
Access:	*Direct access to field from road to south. Network of drainage trenches and mound-planted saplings make access difficult.*
Land:	*Blanket peatland*
Previous Use:	*Rough grazing (sheep)*
Landowner:	*Coillte Teoranta*
SMR No.:	*Not recorded in SMR*

A ring-barrow (in same field as fulacht fiadh) was reported to the Department of Archaeology, UCC, by Coillte Teoranta (Macroom branch). Coillte supplied relevant portion of Ordnance Survey six-inch map with position of site indicated. Site was discovered during planting preparation (1995) when machinery dug through the bank. Work in the immediate area stopped and an area of *c.* 10m around the site was left unplanted. A low wooden stake marks position of the site but as with *fulacht fiadh* in same field (Knocknakilla 1), the stake is not obvious amongst the ground vegetation. Site will be extremely difficult, if not impossible, to access once trees mature.

Ground immediately surrounding site is level, rising to the south and falling gradually to the north. Millstreet County Park is to the east/north-east and 3-5 year plantation is in adjoining field to west/north-west. *Stone enclosure* (CO048-079) in forestry is still visible to the west.

The site was difficult to locate because of the rough ground vegetation but the features are quite obvious in parts, especially in the south and east/north-east sections. Site consists of a circular enclosure (*c.* 19.5m x *c.* 22m) defined by a bank (ext. H *c.* 0.45m; int. H 0.80m) with traces of an outer fosse to south and north/north-east. The north-west section of the enclosure is truncated by a drainage trench and the trees are planted about two metres from that section of the enclosure. The bank at that point is low and less obvious than elsewhere. Presumably it was not noticed by those carrying out the planting.

Outside south-east corner — a small circle of stone paving appears to post-date the ditch but the relationship between the two is not clear.

5. KNOCKNAKILLA (3)

OS 6" Map: *CO 048*

Site Type: *Fulacht Fiadh*

Access: *Direct access from road to South. Network of drainage trenches and mound-planted saplings make access difficult.*

Land: *Blanket peatland*

Previous Use: *Rough grazing (sheep)*

Landowner: *Coillte Teoranta*

SMR No.:   *Not recorded in SMR*

Site was identified during field inspection of circular enclosure and *fulacht fiadh* (see above) reported by Coillte Teoranta. It had not been recognised during planting preparation and was subsequently planted.

Located at a T-junction of two drainage trenches, it is planted with spruce saplings. Identified as semi-oval, peaty mound (*c.* 8m N-S; *c.* 6m E-W; H *c.* 0.7m). Investigation of mound revealed no obvious signs of burnt material and no sign of central depression or 'trough area' normally associated with *fulachta fiadh*. The two drainage trenches, however, cut through mound at south-east where burnt stones (shattered, red and angular) and burnt organic material are evident *c.* 0.2-0.25m beneath peat for *c.* 3m in the trench section.

Two saplings are mound-planted on top of site and drainage trenches have already disturbed it considerably. Coillte has been contacted and asked to remove young saplings from site and area around it. Access will be extremely difficult (if not impossible) once trees mature.

6. CASTLEBLAGH, CO. CORK

OS 6" Map: *CO 034*

Site Type: *Circular Enclosure*

Access: *Direct. 10m in from forest road*

Location: *South of the flood plains along the Blackwater river*

Landowner: *Coillte Teoranta*

SMR No.:   *CO034-046*

Coillte's Environmental Officer (EO) for the Southwest Region, contacted the Department of Archaeology, UCC. The long-established plantation was to be clear-felled and Coillte wanted advice on the best procedure for protecting the site. The EO and the local division Forestry Officer were concerned that extracting the trees would cause further damage to the site. The timber growing on and around the site was a particularly valuable stand of Norway spruce, planted in the 1930s and worth an estimated £5,000. Coillte was prepared to allow the trees remain in place if extraction would prove too damaging.

The site is defined by a large circular, earthen bank (Diam. *c.* 86m NW-SE; int. H *c.* 0.9-2.2m; ext. H *c.* 1.1-3m) surrounded by an external fosse which broadens into an annexe-like feature in south-west section (Cork Archaeological Survey, pers. comm.).

After field inspection and discussion with the EO, it was agreed that the trees would be felled by hand, using a stacking technique whereby the first trees felled would bear the weight and impact of subsequent felling. A section of the site, where the bank and fosse were least obvious, was selected as the extraction route through which the trees would be dragged out. The tree stumps and roots will be left *in situ*. The site and a 10-15m buffer zone will not be replanted by Coillte but natural regeneration (of oak, beech, etc.) is already beginning to take hold and will undoubtedly take over in time.

Appendix 2

An examination of the Inventory database for West Cork and Mid Cork (Power 1992; 1997) was carried out to assess the potential for identifying monuments recorded as being within forestry. Both Inventories list the type of land-use associated with the recorded monuments. It was, therefore, possible to search the database for indications of sites that had been planted and/or were within forestry at the time of inspection.

Details such as the site number, type, height OD, the date on which the site was inspected and the comments regarding the impact of planting on the site, were isolated from the Inventory entries. This resulted in a listing of monuments and potential archaeological sites known to exist, or to have existed, within forestry, including sites which had trees growing in or directly around them.

West Cork Archaeological Inventory:
Sixty-nine sites, either planted and/or within forestry, were noted from the West Cork Inventory. The range of sites affected by planting included megalithic tombs (2), ringforts (38), enclosures (8), burial grounds (2), ring-barrows (2) and standing stones (3). Ten of the sites were inaccessible due to forestry at the time of the visit. The fieldwork for the inventory was carried out between 1983 and 1990, so it is possible that the forestry around some of these sites could have been harvested since. It is, of course, also possible that many more sites have since been planted.

Fifty of the recorded sites were planted with trees, either partially or completely. In one case (Inventory no. 3521) a boulder burial was recorded as having 'roots growing into capstone'.

Mid Cork Archaeological Inventory
One hundred and twenty-six sites from the Inventory of archaeological sites in mid Cork were identified as existing within forestry and/or planted with trees. Seventy-five of these were planted. Sixteen of the recorded sites were inaccessible at the time of visit due to forestry, and six sites were reported as being visibly damaged by forest-related activities. Three *fulachta fiadh* (Inventory nos. 7079, 7080 and 7182) were damaged by drainage trenches. In one case (7079), the burnt material was noted piled around the mound-planted saplings. Two other *fulachta fiadh* (Inventory nos. 7181 and 7182) had been disturbed, with burnt material noted around the base of the tree stems.

Conclusions
One hundred and ninety-five recorded sites were identified as being either within forestry and/or planted with trees. One hundred and twenty of these had trees planted directly on the site. Twenty-six sites were inaccessible due to forestry, and at least eight sites were recorded as having been obviously damaged by forestry related activities.

This very basic search through the Inventory entries was only possible because the survey had recorded the type of land use associated with the monuments. It demonstrated one possible approach to identifying sites that already exist within forestry and that require further site inspection and management. Given that the majority of sites involved were visited during the mid- to late 1980s, it is likely that many more recorded sites in the two regions have since been planted or surrounded by forestry.

Bibliography

AALEN, F.H.A. (ed.) (1985) *The Future of the Irish Rural Landscape*, Department of Geography, Trinity College Dublin.

AALEN, F.H.A., WHELAN, K. and STOUT, M. (1997) *Atlas of the Irish Rural Landscape*, Cork University Press.

ALLEN, F. (1996) 'Forestry Should be Planned', *Irish Farmers Monthly*, May 1996, p. 24.

ANDERSON, E. (1993) 'The Mesolithic: Fishing for Answers', in E. Shee Twohig and M. Ronayne (eds) *Past Perceptions: The Prehistoric Archaeology of South-West Ireland*, Cork University Press, Cork, pp. 16-24.

ANON (1988) 'Community Strategy and Action Programme for the Forestry Sector', Community Communication (COM) 88, 255 final, 23rd Sept. 1988, Brussels.

ANON (a) (1995) 'A Common Forestry Policy: General Survey', European Parliament Directorate General for Research, in Irish Timber Growers Association, *Yearbook and Directory of Services 1995*, ITGA, Dublin, pp. 5-8.

ANON (b) (1995) 'The 1992 Protection of Nature Act in Denmark', Ministry of the Environment, National Forest and Nature Agency, Denmark.

ANON (c) (1995) 'A Statement of Intent between Historic Scotland and Scottish Natural Heritage'.

BARCLAY, G.J. (1992) 'Forestry and Archaeology in Scotland', *Scottish Forestry* 46, pp. 27-47.

BENNETT, I. (ed.) (1995) *Excavations 1994: Summary Accounts of Archaeological Excavations in Ireland*, Wordwell, Co. Wicklow.

BENNETT, I. (ed.) (1996) *Excavations 1995: Summary Accounts of Archaeological Excavations in Ireland*, Wordwell, Co. Wicklow.

BERRY, A.Q. (1992) 'Integrating Archaeology and the Countryside: Clwyd County Council's Approach to ARchaeological Site Management', in L. Macinnes and C.R. Wickham-Jones (eds) *All Natural Things: Archaeology and the Green Debate*, Oxbow Books, Oxford, pp. 155-160.

BERRY, A.Q. (1995) 'Hen Caerwys: A Deserted Medieval Settlement Under Woodland', in Clwyd County Council, *Managing Ancient Monuments: An Integrated Approach*, Clwyd County Council, pp. 105-112.

BOURKE, C. (1995) 'Vow: Bann Drainage Dump' in I. Bennett (ed.) *Excavations 1994: Summary Accounts of Archaeological Excavations in Ireland*, Wordwell, Co. Wicklow, p. 7, no. 9.

BOURKE, C. (1996) 'Ferrystown, Gortgole: Bann Dredgings' in I. Bennett (ed.) *Excavations 1995: Summary Accounts of Archaeological Excavations in Ireland*, Wordwell, Co. Wicklow, p. 2, no. 5.

BRADLEY, K., SKEHAN, C. and WALSH, G. (eds) (1991) *Environmental Impact Assessment: A Technical Approach*, DTPS Environmental Publications, Dublin.

BREEZE, D.J. (1993) 'Ancient Monuments Legislation' in Hunter and Ralston (eds) *Archaeological Resource Management in the UK: An Introduction*, Institute of Field Archaeologists, Birmingham, pp. 44-55.

BUCKLEY, V.M. and SWEETMAN, P.D. (1991) *Archaeological Survey of County Louth*, The Office of Public Works, Dublin.

BULFIN, M. (1992) *Trees on the Farm*, Tree Council of Ireland, Dublin.

BULFIN, M. (1995) 'Starting out in Farm Forestry' in Irish Timber Growers Association, *Yearbook and Directory of Services 1995*, ITGA, Dublin, pp. 37-41.

BULFIN, M., CULLINAN, E.F. and TYNAN, S. (1993) 'The Development of an Indicative Forest Strategy with Specific Reference to Co. Clare', *Irish Forestry*, Vol. 50, No. 1, pp. 98.

BYRNES, E. (1992) 'Forestry Development: The EIA Process and Archaeology: Present Practice and Proposals for Future Development', Diploma in EIA Management Project (unpublished), Department of Archaeology, University College Dublin.

CARVER, M. (1996) 'On archaeological value' *Antiquity*, Vol. 70, No. 267, pp. 45-56.

CAULFIELD, S. (1983) 'The Neolithic Settlement of North Connaught' in T. Reeves-Smith and F. Hamond (eds) *Landscape Archaeology in Ireland*, BAR (British Series) 116, Oxford, pp. 195-216.

CLEARY, R.M. (1993) 'The Later Bronze Age at Lough Gur: Filling in the Blanks', in E. Shee Twohig and M. Ronayne (eds) *Past Perceptions: The Prehistoric Archaeology of South-West Ireland*, Cork University Press, Cork, pp. 114-120.

CLEARY, R.M., HURLEY, M.F. and TWOHIG, E. (1987) *Archaeological Excavations on the Cork-Dublin Gas Pipeline (1981-1982)*, Cork Archaeological Studies No. 1, University College Cork.

CLWYD COUNTY COUNCIL (1995) *Managing Ancient Monuments: An Integrated Approach*, Clwyd County Council.

COILLTE TEORANTA (1992a) 'Coomacheo, Ballyvourney, Co. Cork', Environmental Impact Statement, Coillte Teoranta, Dublin.

COILLTE TEORANTA (1992b) *Discovering Ireland's Woodlands: A Guide to Forest Parks, Picnic Sites and Woodland Walks*, Coillte Teoranta, Dublin.

COILLTE TEORANTA (1993) 'Environmental Policy Statement of Coillte', Coillte Teoranta, Dublin.

COILLTE TEORANTA (1994) 'Annual Report and Accounts 1993', Coillte Teoranta, Dublin.

CONDIT, T. (1991) 'Archaeology' in K. Bradley, C. Skeehan and G. Walsh (eds) *Environmental Impact Assessment: A Technical Approach*, DTPS Environmental Publications, Dublin, pp. 111-115.

CONDIT, T. (1997) *Ireland's Archaeology from the Air*, Dublin.

CONDIT, T. and O'SULLIVAN, A. (1995) 'A Later Prehistoric Settlement Complex at Knockroe, Co. Limerick', *IAPA News Letter*, No. 21, pp. 5-7.

COONEY, G. (1991) 'The Archaeological Endowment' in J. Feehan (ed.) *Environment and Development in Ireland*, The Environmental Institute, University College Dublin, pp. 70-80.

COONEY, G. (1993) 'Forestry and the Cultural Landscape: Understanding the Past in the Present' *Irish Forestry*, 1993, Vol. 50, No. 1, pp. 13-19.

COUNCIL OF EUROPE (1992) *European Convention on the Protection of the Archaeological Heritage (revised)*, European Treaty Series 143, Valletta.

COUNCIL OF EUROPE (1993) *Protection of Archaeological Heritage: Explanatory Report on the Revised Convention Opened for Signature on 16 January 1992*, Council of Europe Press, Strasbourg.

CUPPAGE, J. (1986) *Archaeological Survey of the Dingle Peninsula*, Ballyferriter.

DARVILL, T. (1986) *Upland Archaeology: What Future for the Past?*, Council for British Archaeology, HMSO, London.

DAVID, A. (1995) 'Geophysical Survey in Archaeological Field Evaluation', *English Heritage, Research and Professional Services Guideline*, No. 1, London.

de BUITLÉAR, É. (1995) *Ireland's Wild Countryside*, Tiger Books, London.

DEMPSEY, M. (1995) 'Forestry and Land Use Policy' in Irish Timber Growers Association, *Yearbook and Directory of Services 1995*, ITGA, Dublin, pp. 20-26.

D/ANI (1993) *Afforestation: The DANI Statement on Environmental Policy*, Department of Agriculture for Northern Ireland Communications Unit, HMSO, Belfast.

D/AFF (Department of Agriculture, Food and Forestry) (1992) *Rural Environment Protection Scheme: Farm Development Service: Agri-Environmental Specifications*, Stationery Office, Dublin.

D/AFF (Department of Agriculture, Food and Forestry) (1994a) *Operational Programme for Agriculture, Rural Development and Forestry, 1994-1999*, Stationery Office, Dublin.

D/AFF (Department of Agriculture, Food and Forestry) (1994b) 'Afforestation Grant Scheme/Forest Premium Scheme', Department of Agriculture, Food and Forestry, Dublin.

D/AFF (Department of Agriculture, Food and Forestry) (1996) *Growing for the Future: A Strategic Plan for the Development of the Forestry Sector in Ireland*, Stationery Office, Dublin.

DOODY, M.G. (1987) 'Curraghatoor, Co. Tipperary. Hut Sites' in R.M. Cleary, M.F. Hurley and E. Twohig (eds) *Archaeological excavations on the Cork-Dublin Gas Pipeline (1981-82)*, Cork Archaeological Studies No. 1, University College Cork, pp. 36-42.

DOODY, M.G. (1993) 'Bronze Age Settlement', in E. Shee Twohig and M. Ronayne (eds) *Past Perceptions: The Prehistoric Archaeology of South-West Ireland*, Cork University Press, Cork, pp. 93-100.

DUNSTAN, G. (1985) 'Forests in the Landscape' in F.H.A. Aalen (ed.) *The Future of the Irish Rural Landscape*, Department of Geography, Trinity College Dublin, pp. 93-153.

EUROPEAN PARLIAMENT (1983) 'Resolution on the Protection of Irish Bogs', *Official Journal of the European Communities*, No. C 96/95, 11th April.

FAO REPORT (1951) 'Report on Forestry Mission to Ireland', Food and Agriculture Organisation of the United Nations, Stationery Office, Dublin.

FARRELL, E.P. (1993) 'Editorial', *Irish Forestry*, Vol. 50, No. 1.

FARRELL, E.P. and BOYLE, G. (1990) 'Peatland Forestry in the 1990s', *Irish Forestry*, Vol. 47 (2), pp. 69-78.

FARRELL, E.P. and KELLY-QUINN, M. (1991) 'Forestry and the Environment', in J. Feehan (ed.) *Environment and Development in Ireland*, The Environmental Institute, University College Dublin, pp. 353-357.

FEEHAN, J. (ed.) (1991) *Environment and Development in Ireland*, The Environmental Institute, University College Dublin.

FOLEY, C., GIBBONS, M. and STOUT, G. (1991) 'Forestry and Archaeology' Report produced by the Subcommittee on Forestry and Archaeology, Irish Association of Professional Archaeologists, April 1991.

FORAIOSE don BPOBAL (FORESTRY for COMMUNITY) 'A Draft Proposal for Submission to the Minister for Forestry and Rural Development', unpublished document.

FOREST SERVICE a 'Forestry and Archaeology Guidelines', Forest Service, Dublin.

FOREST SERVICE b 'Forestry and the Landscape Guidelines', Forest Service, Dublin.

FORESTRY COMMISSION (1995) 'Forests and Archaeological Guidelines', Forestry Commission, Edinburgh.

GAFFNEY, C., GATER, J. and OVENDEN, S. (1991) 'The Use of Geophysical Techniques in Archaeological Evaluations', *Institute of Field Archaeologists, Technical Paper*, No. 9.

GALLAGHER, L. (1995) 'Links in the Timber Chain in the Republic of Ireland', in Irish Timber Growers Association, *Yearbook and Directory of Services 1995*, ITGA, Dublin, pp. 12-18.

GARDINER, J.J. (1991) 'Forest Production — Quality or Quantity?', in J. Feehan (ed.) *Environment and Development in Ireland*, The Environmental Institute, University College Dublin, pp. 348-352.

GOODSTADT, V. (1991) 'Indicative Forestry Strategies: the Scottish Experience', in C. Mollan and M. Maloney (eds) *The Right Trees in the Right Places*, Royal Dublin Society, Dublin.

GROGAN, E. (1991) 'Neolithic Settlements', in M. Ryan (ed.) *The Illustrated Archaeology of Ireland*, Country House, Dublin, pp. 59-63.

GROGAN, E., CONDIT, T., O'CARROLL, F. and O'SULLIVAN, A. (1995) 'Preliminary Assessment of the Prehistoric Landscape of the Mooghaun Study Area', in *Discovery Programme Reports 2: Project Results 1993*, Royal Irish Academy, Dublin, pp. 47-56.

HALLIDAY, S.P. and RITCHIE, J.N.G. (1992) 'The Afforestable Land Survey: Royal Commission on the Ancient and Historical Monuments of Scotland' in L. Macinnes and C.R. Wickham-Jones (eds) *All Natural Things: Archaeology and the Green Debate*, Oxbow Books, Oxford, pp. 169-175.

HAYFIELD, C. (ed.) (1980) *Field Walking as a Method of Archaeological Research*, Directorate of Ancient Monuments and Historic Buildings, Occasional Papers No. 2, DOE, London.

HEDLEY, S. (ed.) (1993) *Rescuing the Historic Environment*, RESCUE.

HERITAGE SERVICE (1997) *National Monuments Acts 1930-94: Advice Notes on Excavation Licences*, National Monuments and Historic Properties Service, Dublin.

HICKIE, D. (1990) *Forestry in Ireland: Policy and Practice*, An Taisce, Dublin.

HICKIE, D., TURNER, R., MELLON, C. and COVENEY, J. (1993) *Ireland's Forested Future: A Plan for Forestry and the Environment*, Royal Society for the Protection of Birds, An Taisce and the Irish Wildbird Conservancy, Dublin.

HICKIE, D. (1994) 'A National Land Use Policy — Could it Work?' *Living Heritage*, Vol. 11, No. 2, pp. 2-3.

HUMMEL (1983) 'Trees in the Evolution of the European Landscape' in *Trees in the 21st Century*, AB Academic Publications, 1983.

HUNTER and RALSTON (eds) (1993) *Archaeological Resource Management in the UK: An Introduction*, Institute of Field Archaeologists, Birmingham.

IAPA (Irish Association of Professional Archaeologists) (1994) 'Strategy for the Development of the Forestry Sector in Ireland' (Unpublished document).

IAPA (Irish Association of Professional Archaeologists) (1995) 'IAPA: Towards Adoption of Guidelines, Procedures and Standards for the Professional Practice of Archaeology' *IAPA News Letter*, No. 20.

IRISH FARMERS' ASSOCIATION (1995) 'Land Use Policy', IFA proposal to Government, Jan. 1995.

IRISH PEATLAND CONSERVATION COUNCIL (1989) 'Irish Peatland Conservation Programme: IPCC Action Plan 1989-1992', Irish Peatland Conservation Council, Dublin.

IRISH TIMBER GROWERS ASSOCIATION (1995) *Yearbook and Directory of Services 1995*, ITGA, Dublin.

KEARNEY, B. (1995) 'The Impact of Forestry on Rural Communities: Land Availability for Forestry', in Irish Timber Growers Association, *Yearbook and Directory of Services 1995*, ITGA, Dublin, pp. 27-30.

KEELEY, V.J. (1996) 'Ballydavis, Co. Laois' in I. Bennett (ed.) *Excavations in Ireland 1995*, pp. 51-2, no. 173.

KELLEHER, M. (1993) 'Lime Kiln, Derreenaling Townland, Ballyvourney, Co. Cork — Relocated Aug/Sept 1993' (Unpublished report).

KELLEHER, M.G. (1995) 'An Investigation of Field Systems and Enclosures in Counties Limerick and Clare using Analytical Aerial Photography', MA Thesis (unpublished) Department of Archaeology, University College Cork.

KIRWAN, S. (1993) 'The Limerick Sites and Monuments Record: A Means for Reviewing the Current State of Research', in E. Shee Twohig and M. Ronayne (eds) *Past Perceptions: The Prehistoric Archaeology of South-West Ireland*, Cork University Press, Cork, pp. 140-146.

KRISTIANSEN, K. (1988) 'Nature and Culture in the National Forest and Nature Agency', *Antikvariske Studier* 9.

KRISTIANSEN, K. (1992) 'From Romanticism, Through Antiquarianism, to an Historical View of Nature: The Case of Denmark', in L. Macinnes and C.R. Wickham-Jones (eds) *All Natural Things: Archaeology and the Green Debate*, Oxbow Books, Oxford, pp. 52-64.

LACY, B. (1983) *Archaeological Survey of County Donegal*, Donegal County Council, Lifford.

LAMBRICK, G. (1992) 'The Importance of the Cultural Heritage in a Green World: Towards the Development of Landscape', in L. Macinnes and C.R. Wickham-Jones (eds) *All Natural Things: Archaeology and the Green Debate*, Oxbow Books, Oxford, pp. 105-126.

LEE, G. (1995) 'Forestry Management and Archaeology', in Clwyd County Council, *Managing Ancient Monuments: An Integrated Approach*, Clwyd County Council, pp. 97-105.

MACINNES, L. (1993) 'Archaeology as Land Use', in Hunter and Ralston (eds) *Archaeological Resource Management in the UK: An Introduction*, Institute of Field Archaeologists, Birmingham, pp. 243-255.

MACINNES, L. and WICKHAM-JONES, C.R. (eds) (1992a) *All Natural Things: Archaeology and the Green Debate*, Oxbow Books, Oxford.

MACINNES, L. and WICKHAM-JONES, C.R. (eds) (1992b) 'Time-depth in the Countryside: Archaeology and the Environment', in L. Macinnes and C.R. Wickham-Jones (eds) *All Natural Things: Archaeology and the Green Debate*, Oxbow Books, Oxford, pp. 1-13.

McCORMACK, A. and O'LEARY, T. (1993) 'Classification of Landscape Sensitivity for Visual Impact Assessment of Forestry', *Irish Forestry*, Vol. 50, No. 1, pp. 1-12.

McLOUGHLIN, J. (1997) 'Fitting the Forests into the Landscape', in T. O'Regan (ed.) *Irish Landscape Forum: The Second Landfall*, Landscape Alliance Ireland, Cork, pp. 42-46.

MERCER, R.J. (1980) 'Archaeological Field Survey in Northern Scotland 1976-1979', Department of Archaeology, University of Edinburgh, Occasional Papers 4, Edinburgh.

MITCHELL, F. (1976) *The Irish Landscape*, Collins, London.

MITCHELL, G.F. and RYAN, M. (1997) *Reading the Irish Landscape*, Town House, Dublin.

MOLLAN, C. and MALONEY, M. (eds) (1991) *The Right Trees in the Right Places*, Royal Dublin Society, Dublin.

MORGAN EVANS, D. (1985) 'The Management of Historic Landscapes' in Lambrick *Archaeology and Nature Conservation*, Oxford University Department of External Studies, Oxford, pp. 89-94.

MOUNT, C. (1996) 'The Environmental Siting of Neolithic and Bronze Age Monuments in the Bricklieve and Moytirra Uplands, Co. Sligo' *The Journal of Irish Archaeology*, Vol. 7, pp. 1-11.

MULLOY, F. (1991) 'Forestry Development: Review of Existing and Prospective EC Policies and Implementation' in Feehan, J (ed.) *Environment and Development in Ireland*, The Environmental Institute, University College Dublin, pp. 340-347.

MULLOY, F. (1995) 'Forestry Research: Pathway to Progress' in Irish Timber Growers Association *Yearbook and Directory of Services 1995*, ITGA, Dublin, pp. 33-34.

NEESON, E. (1991) *A History of Irish Forestry*, The Lilliput Press, Dublin.

O'CARROLL, N. (ed.) (1984) *The Forests of Ireland*, The Society of Irish Foresters, Dublin.

O'CONNELL, M. (1991) 'The Environment and Human Activity in Bronze Age Ireland' in M. Ryan (ed.) *The Illustrated Archaeology of Ireland*, Country House, Dublin, pp. 66-67.

OFFICE OF PUBLIC WORKS (1990) *Killarney National Park: Management Plan*, Stationery Office, Dublin.

O'HALLORAN, J. and GILLER, P.S. (1993) 'Forestry and the Ecology of Streams and Rivers: Lessons from Abroad?' *Irish Forestry*, Vol. 50, No. 1, pp. 35-52.

Ó NUALLÁIN, S. (1972) 'A Neolithic house at Ballyglass near Ballycastle, Co. Mayo' *Journal of the Royal Society of Antiquarians Ireland*, 102, pp. 49-57.

O'REGAN, T. (1994) 'The Case for a National Landscape Policy', Submission document to Government (unpublished).

O'REGAN, T. (ed.) (1996) *Irish Landscape Forum '95*, Landscape Alliance Ireland, Cork.

O'REGAN, T. (ed.) (1997) *Irish Landscape Forum: The Second Landfall*, Landscape Alliance Ireland, Cork.

Ó RÍORDÁIN, S.P. (1954) 'Lough Gur Excavations: Neolithic and Bronze Age houses on Knockadoon', *Proceedings of the Royal Irish Academy* 56C, pp. 297-459.

O'SULLIVAN, A. and SHEEHAN, J. (1993) 'The South West Kerry Archaeological Field Survey' in E. Shee Twohig and M. Ronayne (eds) *Past Perceptions: The Prehistoric Archaeology of South-West Ireland*, Cork University Press, Cork, pp. 147-148.

O'SULLIVAN, A. and SHEEHAN, J. (1996) *The Iveragh Peninsula: An Archaeological Survey of South Kerry*, Cork University Press, Cork.

PIEDA (1986) 'Forestry in Great Britain: An Economic Assessment for the National Audit Office', NAO, London.

POWER, D. (1988) 'Aerial Photography and Regional Survey', *Organisation of Irish Archaeologists' Newsletter*, No. 7, pp. 16-17.

POWER, D. (1992) *Archaeological Inventory of County Cork: Volume 1: West Cork*, The Office of Public Works, Dublin.

POWER, D. (1993) 'Archaeological Survey in the Republic of Ireland and the Cork Experience' in E. Shee Twohig and M. Ronayne (eds) *Past Perceptions: The Prehistoric Archaeology of South-West Ireland*, Cork University Press, Cork, pp. 137-139.

POWER, D. (1994) *Archaeological Inventory of County Cork: Volume 2: East and South Cork*, The Office of Public Works, Dublin.

POWER, D. (1997) *Archaeological Inventory of County Cork: Volume 3: Mid Cork*, The Office of Public Works, Dublin.

POWER, D., BYRNE, E., EGAN, U., LANE, S. and SLEEMAN, M. (1988) *Sites and Monuments Records County Cork: A List of Archaeological Sites in Co. Cork*, Vols. 1, 2 and 3, Office of Public Works and Department of Archaeology, University College Cork.

PROUDFOOT, E. (ed.) (1989) 'Our Vanishing Heritage: Forestry and Archaeology', *Council for Scottish Archaeology, Occasional Papers, 2*, Edinburgh.

REEVES-SMITH, T. and HAMOND, F. (eds) (1983) *Landscape Archaeology in Ireland*, BAR (British Series) 116, Oxford.

RCAHMS (Royal Commission on the Ancient and Historic Monuments of Scotland) (1993) *Strath of Kildonan: An Archaeological Survey*, RCAHMS, Edinburgh.

RYAN, M. (1980) 'An Early Mesolithic Site in the Irish Midlands', *Antiquity*, No. 54, pp. 46-47.

RYAN, M. (ed.) (1991) *The Illustrated Archaeology of Ireland*, Country House, Dublin.

RYNNE, C. (1993) *The Archaeology of Cork City and Harbour from the Earliest Times to Industrialisation*, Collins Press, Cork.

SCANLAN, H. (1995) 'Forestry', in *Irish Farmers' Journal*, October 21st, 1995, pp. 41-48.

SHEE TWOHIG, E. and RONAYNE, M. (eds) (1993) *Past Perceptions: The Prehistoric Archaeology of South-West Ireland*, Cork University Press, Cork.

SHEPHERD, I.A.G. (1992) 'The Friendly Forester? Archaeology, Forestry and the Green Movement' in L. Macinnes and C.R. Wickham-Jones (eds) *All Natural Things: Archaeology and the Green Debate*, Oxbow Books, Oxford, pp. 161-168.

STOUT, G., FITZPATRICK, E., DALY, K., DUNFORD, P. and FARRELLY, J. (1990) *Sites and Monuments Record, County Kerry: A List of Archaeological Sites in Co. Kerry*, Office of Public Works, Dublin.

TITHE AN OIREACHTAIS (1997) *Seventh Joint Committee on State-Sponsored Bodies: 5th Report: Coillte Teoranta*, Government of Ireland, Dublin.

TOMLINSON, R. (1997) 'Forests and Woodland' in F.H.A. Aalen, K. Whelan and M. Stout (eds) *Atlas of the Irish Rural Landscape*, Cork University Press, Cork, pp. 122-133.

WALKER, W.B. (1986) 'Private Forestry in the UK' *Irish Forestry*, Vol. 43, No. 2, pp. 116-121.

WILLIAMS, B.B. (1986) 'Excavations at Altanagh, Co. Tyrone', *Ulster Journal of Archaeology* 49, pp. 33-88.

WOODMAN, P.C. and O'BRIEN, M. (1993) 'Excavations at Ferriter's Cove, Co. Kerry: An Interim Statement' in E. Shee Twohig and M. Ronayne (eds) *Past Perceptions: The Prehistoric Archaeology of South-West Ireland*, Cork University Press, Cork, pp. 25-34.

YARNELL, T. (1993) 'Archaeological Conservation in Woods and Forests' in S. Hedley (ed.) *Rescuing the Historic Environment*, RESCUE, pp. 29-30.

ZVELEBIL, M., MOORE, J.A., GREEN, S.W. and HENDERSON, D. (1987) 'Regional Survey and the Analysis of Lithic Scatters: A case study from Southeast Ireland' in P. Rowley-Conwy, M. Zvelebil and H.P. Blankholm (eds) *Mesolithic Northwest Europe: Recent Trends*, Sheffield, pp. 9-32.